Killough

THE CHURCH ON THE LOUGH

Aspects of village history and collected stories

by

Christine Walsh, Margaret Manley,
Finbar McCormick and Harry Madill

The Palatine Trust

Published by
The Palatine Trust
38 Castle Street
Killough
Co. Down
BT39 7QQ
May 2000

ISBN 0-9538528-0-6

Designed by December Publications

Printed by Graham & Heslip

Publication financed by COAST-Heritage European Commission Programme
and Down District Council

Front cover: Killough Bay by Jim Manley
Back cover: Scordon and yawls by Johnnie McSherry 1885
courtesy of Tom McClean, Killough

CONTENTS

Introduction   7

Part 1:   Killough – The Church by the Lough by Christine Walsh and Margaret Manley   9

Part 2:   Aspects of Killough History by Finbar McCormick

    A Killough Soldier's Tale   53

    A Killough Sailor's Tale   58

    The Early Pier in Killough   71

    The Early Years of the Primary Schools at Killough   76

    Charles Sheils and his Almshouses   80

    The Killough Lifeboat   83

Part 3:   The Killough Yawl by Harry Madill   104

INTRODUCTION

This book presents and brings together a series of essays dealing with the history of Killough. It continues the documentation of the village that has already begun with the publication of Maurice Hayes' wonderful *Sweet Killough let go your anchor*, a memoir of the village in the 1930s. It is produced as part of the COAST-Heritage European Commission Programme in partnership with Down District Council. The book is divided into three parts.

The first part consists of a reprint of *The Church by the Lough* written by Christina Walsh and Margaret Manley to celebrate Killough Village Festival of 1990. The authors state that 'the book is a brief history and collection of stories from bygone days, stories which could have been lost forever. It is not intended to be an academic historical document'. As it was written over a decade ago it is inevitable that a few aspects of the text are out of date. Some of those who were alive at the time of it compilation are now deceased, the brickworks are now closed and the marina that was to have been built in Killough was instead located at Ardglass.

The second part, by Finbar McCormick consists of some chapters dealing with various aspects of the history of Killough mostly concerning its maritime past.

The final part, by Harry Madill, deals with the history of the Killough Yawl. It is a reprint of an article first published in Down Museum's Journal, *Down Survey*, Vol. 2, and is reproduced with their kind permission.

Many people helped with the preparation of this volume, especially in the provision of illustrations and for allowing their reproduction, and for allowing us to quote from documents in their possession. For this we would like to thank Alex Carroll, Malcolm Collins, Joe McClean, Tom McClean, Down County Museum, the Deputy Keeper of Records, Public Record Office of Northern Ireland (D/642/G1 and D/671/C147/1-18), Mary Duffy, Les Jones, Imelda Keeling, Josie Kernahan, Tony Merrick, Paul Stewart, and especially the late Cecily Parkinson-Cumine. Every effort has been made to contact the copyright owners of the postcards used in this book. If anyone has been overlooked could they please contact the Palatine Trust.

The front cover illustration was kindly provided by Jim Manley.

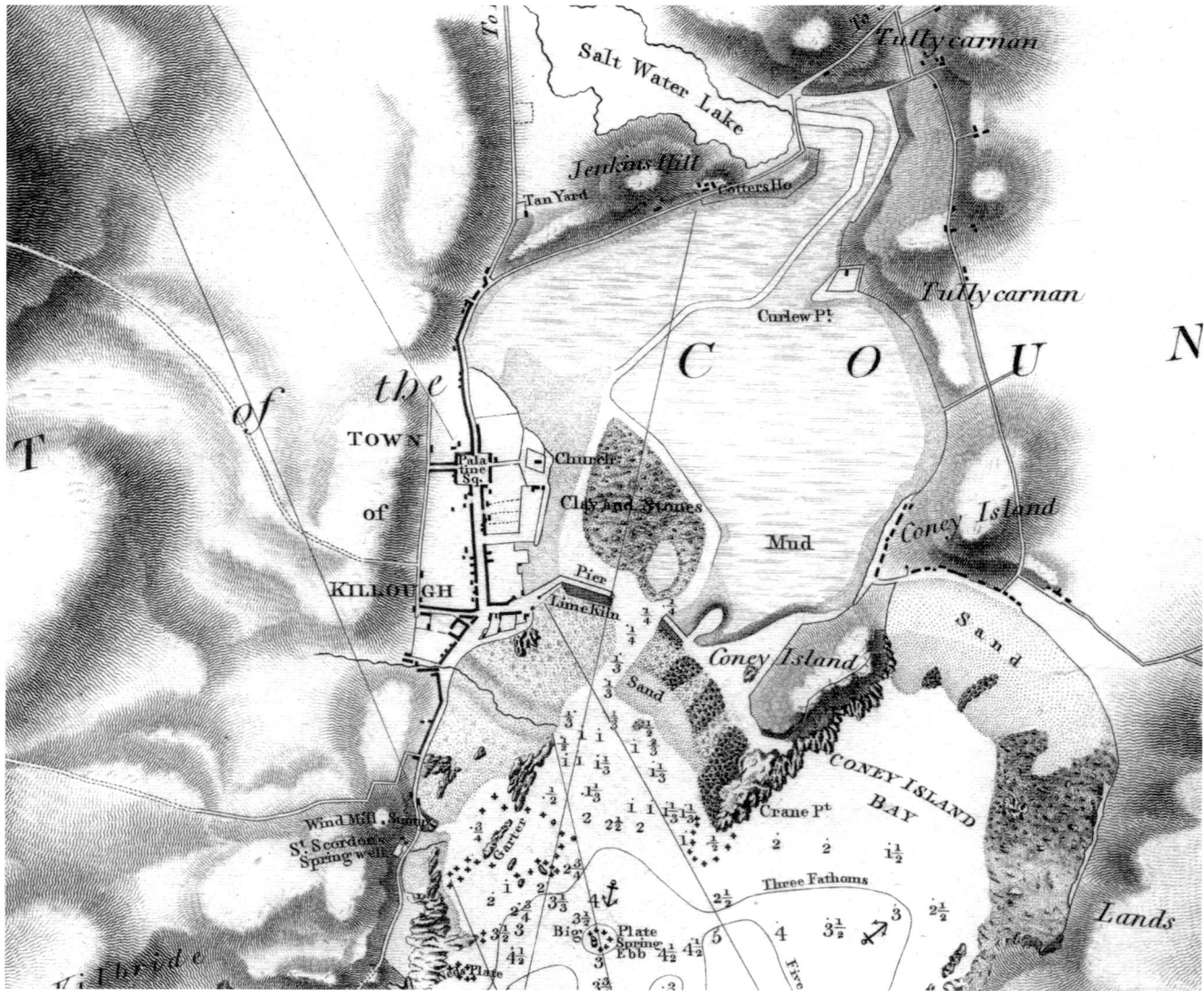

Alexander Nimmo's Map of Killough, 1821

THE HISTORY OF KILLOUGH

Castle Street (Hunter's Store) circa 1890

Killough, 'The Garden of Ireland': That is how G.H. Bassett described the village in his County Down Guide of 1886. Throughout history the village of Killough has inspired visitors to comment favourably upon its beauty. No one could fail to be impressed by the stately avenue of sycamore trees that lines the main thoroughfare, lending an almost continental flavour to the village. The sweeping curve of the bay, the Ropewalk and many attractive buildings make Killough one of the prettiest villages in Lecale. Killough was named from the Irish Cill Locha, which means church on the lough.

Towards the end of the twelfth century the Normans invaded Ireland. The Lecale was conquered by the army of a particular knight, Sir John De Courcy, who instigated the building of some of the castles to be found in this area. King Henry II of England divided Ireland into counties and his son, King John, further divided the counties into Baronies. The Barony of Lecale contained the county town of Downpatrick, Dundrum, Strangford and Killough.

After the coming of De Courcy in 1177 and the settling of the Anglo-Normans, the lands of

Killough passed into the hands of the Russell family. The Russells of Killough were descended from a member of the house of Kingston-Russell, a companion of De Courcy. Thomas Russell was granted the Barony of Killough in 1316 during the reign of Edward II of England. He was succeeded by a long line of descendants, who became Gaelicised through inter-marriage to members of the Magennis, Macarton and O'Neil families.

Another Thomas Russell was the fifth baron of Killough and a Richard Russell was Grand Justiciary of Ulster in the reign of Richard II (1377-1399). During the reign of Henry IV, (1399-1413) George Russell, the baron of Killough at that time, petitioned the King for aid to defend Killough against marauders from Scotland and the neighbouring families of Magennis, O'Neil and Macarton. Killough was an area desired by many of the prominent families in the Lecale at that time, therefore, during their period of ownership the Russell family were faced with many dilemmas. Not only did they have to protect their territory from attack by neighbouring clans, they also had to contend with oppression from England.

In 1600 Lord Mountjoy was commanded by Elizabeth I to bring the chiefs of Ulster to heel. He did this by mounting the biggest military operation Ireland had ever seen. The fact that his predecessor, the Earl of Essex, had failed to control Ulster and had been returned to England for execution, no doubt added to the fervour with which Mountjoy set out to accomplish his task.

A huge army of foot and horse soldiers marched through Lecale. Fynes Morrison records:

Main Street, Killough
circa 1920

"The 16th. day His Lordship marched with the army...to Dundrum. There Phelim McEvir Magennis submitted himself and yielded to the queen his castle in Dundrum. The next day His Lordship ...rode to Ardglass... Two castles surrendered the garrisons and yielded up their arms... After dinner His Lordship rode to Russell's Town (Killough). Thus Mountjoy secured Lecale for the crown."

The Russells, having chosen allegiance to the Irish against Mountjoy during this campaign, expected to be punished and dispossessed of their lands, but were granted a pardon in 1602, retaining ownership of Killough.

In the early part of the seventeenth century much of the Lecale was owned by the Cromwell family. Other families new to the area were the Hamiltons and the Wards. These new families got on reasonably well with the already established land-owning families, such as the Russells, and although they practised different religions this did not create any serious barrier between them. Indeed, Elinor, daughter of Richard Russell married Nicholas Ward of Castleward, thus uniting an established Catholic family with a new Protestant family.

Unfortunately for the Russell family religion in the mid-seventeenth century became a test of loyalty to the Crown. Unable to accept the 39 Articles of the Established Church of England or the Act of Uniformity they allied themselves to the 'Old English' of the Lecale and chose to defy the Crown. They were leading rebels in the uprising of 1641 and were duly punished for their part. They were dispossessed of their lands and their estates were consequently broken up. John, the 12th. Baron

Killough in a storm, circa 1950

of Killough, lost his lands to Robert Hammond and the Duke of York, who later became James II. Robert Hammond sold his land to Sir Robert Ward of Castleward and when James II lost the throne in 1688, the Government sold off his Lecale lands. Sir Robert Ward then became the owner of 8,000 acres of the best land in the barony and the port of Killough.

The Ward family originally came to County Down in the latter half of the 16th century when land in Strangford was purchased from the Earl of Kildare by Bernard Ward, a native of Capesthorne in Cheshire. Bernard was the father of Sir Robert Ward, the Surveyor General of Ireland. The estate at that time was called Carrick na Sheannagh, later to be named Castleward.

Bernard's great-grandson, Bernard Ward, was High Sheriff of County Down. He fought a duel with his cousin, Jocelyn Hamilton, in October 1690. At this time all Catholic priests had been ordered to leave Ireland. That they did not all do so led to Jocelyn Hamilton being accused by his cousin, Bernard Ward, of assisting a priest to escape. In the Grand Jury Room while attending Down Assizes,

Bernard taunted Jocelyn about the matter. According to local tradition, the duel took place in the hollow now occupied by the Southwell School. Jocelyn Hamilton was getting the better of the sword fight when Bernard Ward opened fire with a pistol that he had concealed upon his person. As Jocelyn Hamilton was shot he cried out "Foul stroke, Cousin Ward" and leaping forward he made a home thrust with his sword, piercing Bernard through almost to the hilt. Such a double murder should have shocked the entire community, but the violence of the times set against a background of warfare of the two previous years, demonstrates the savagery of the times.

The Bernard Ward killed in the duel was the father of Michael Ward, to whom Killough owed much for its prosperity as it flourished throughout the 18th century. Michael Ward became Justice of the King's Bench in 1725. He was a shrewd businessman and an active promoter of the linen trade. When he inherited Killough he developed a thriving port by building a strong quay and creating a safe harbour. Prior to his land-lordship there appears to have been little or no development in Killough.

He changed the name of the town from Killough to Port St. Anne in honour of his wife, Anne (nee Hamilton), who was extremely fond of the town. It is said that she was so fond of visiting the town from her home at Castleward near Strangford, that her husband commissioned the long, straight road to make her journeys more easily accomplished. However, it is more likely that the roads were built for the transportation of lead, mined in Castleward and exported from Killough, because the majority of roads at that time were little better than cart tracks.

Not only was Michael Ward a conscientious husband, he was also a caring landlord, for it was he who first saw the potential of the harbour and had built the strong quay where ships could lie safely at anchor. Fifteen boats belonged to the port, plying foreign and domestic trade. Barley was the chief export whilst commodities were being imported for distribution throughout the county.

The manufacture of salt was yet another of Michael Ward's innovations and this was greatly assisted by the infrequent number of fresh water rivers that run into the salt water along the shoreline. No streams of any magnitude flow into the bay, thus making the salinity of the waters ideal for this type of manufacture. Mr Ward, along with his younger brother Robert, established the salt works which functioned for many years. Apparently the venture was fraught with problems and appears to have not been a very profitable one. Its inability to make a profit seems to have been further hampered by the lack of a willing labour force, for in a letter written in 1724 by William Montgomery, a partner of Michael Ward and joint owner of the sailing ship the 'Successful', he commented:

> 'Successful which came loaded with coals near a fortnight ago is not yet half discharged, there not being above four or five labourers in town has cart and horses and they are so perversely lazy they will work only ye times or hours they please.'

The 'Successful' appears not to have quite lived up to her name. In letters from William Montgomery to Michael Ward references were made to lost cargoes and the importation of poor cargoes. In a letter dated May 25th 1726 Montgomery reports of a cargo of timber.

"So bad that in all my life I never saw such rubbish. John Mahood says as dus many more its excessive dear at £1. 5s per tun, a great part of it is so rotten it would not even be firewood, being vile and crukitt dirt."

Smuggling too caused the Wards a problem. They objected to the smuggling in of tobacco aboard their ships, but were unable to prevent this to any extent. It would appear that the cargo shipping business was also fraught with problems. Robert Ward found it necessary to arm the port against 'Privateers.' He considered them such a menace that he wrote,

"If we have not a few guns of five or six pounders a privateer may not only take every ship out of our harbour but may beat down the town of Killough."

A further letter tells of guns taken from a sunken ship lost in Killough Bay, that may have been the old guns which for many years lay rusting on Killough quay and later used as bollards.

Under the management of a man called Lascelles (a name still connected with this area) the salt works continued to trade. A malthouse was erected for the brewing of beer and the inhabitants of Killough were instructed to buy their malt beer from this establishment only and not from other breweries in Down. This was just one of the many ways in which the Ward family continued to influence life in Killough.

About this same time Mr. Michael Ward also

Mill Hill, circa 1920

erected a Charter Working School for the employment of "20 poor Popish children" who were to be trained in useful labour and carefully educated in the principles of the Protestant religion. Some of these children were brought in from "the remote parts of the kingdom the better to preserve them from the influence of their Popish relations". They were chiefly employed in the manufacture of linen and a workhouse and looms were set up. They cultivated the land around the school to grow their own vegetables and flax. The flax was spun into fine linen cloth. Some of the boys were sent to sea and others were apprenticed to local farmers and linen weavers.

The wealthy merchants and the ship owners built fine houses in the Square and along Castle Street. Their warehouses and grain stores were built along Quay Lane and in the area where Castle Court stands today. There were at least nine large grain stores in Killough, many of which had kilns attached, to dry the grain.

Whilst larger boats carried out the business of trade about twenty smaller boats were employed in the fishing industry. There was a plentiful supply of cod, ling, whiting, mackerel and herring. Lobsters and crabs were also in abundance. About fifty men were employed as fishermen and this, and many other business enterprises, provided most of the inhabitants of Killough with employment during the 18th Century.

In 1781 the Ward family were advanced to the peerage and Michael Ward's son, yet another Bernard, became the first Viscount Bangor. In 1821 Lord Bangor, the 3rd Viscount, commissioned Alexander Nimmo to build a harbour in Killough. The original quay, built in Michael Ward's time, was no longer adequate for the amount of trade in and out of the port. The harbour cost £18,000, a princely sum in those days. Two piers were erected on either side of the bay. The pier on the Killough side of the bay was about five hundred feet long and the Coney Island pier was about one hundred feet in length. These piers were built of granite and blackstone dressed with sandstone copings. An attractive tower was placed at the end of each pier.

Not only was the harbour pleasing to the eye, it was described in several documents written in the following fifty years after its completion, as

"the most commodious safe haven on the County Down coast. It has safe berths for merchant ships of a hundred and fifty tons fully laden and has the added advantage of depth of ten to eighteen feet at high water."

Throughout the remainder of the nineteenth century Killough was a busy and thriving port. It was the principal point of export for the grain growing county of Lecale, the chief export being barley. Potatoes were also exported in great quantity and coal was the chief import. The harbour area afforded opportunity for small scale boat building to be carried out. Fishing vessels too used the harbour. Killough was indeed a lively and enterprising town.

Therefore it is difficult to imagine a time when Killough had only 21 inhabitants, yet when Pender compiled his Census of Ireland in 1650 he recorded a population of that number; 10 of these inhabitants were Irish and 11 were English and Scottish settlers. Even to this day Killough appeals to those from other shores.

As trade and industry increased so did the population. The prospect of regular employment in a pleasing environment attracted many to settle in Killough over the next two hundred years.

The Parliamentary Gazetteer of 1846 records the following facts:

Population:	1148
Houses:	224
Families employed in agriculture:	51
Manufacturers and trade:	126
Others:	81
Families dependent on property and professions:	21
On the directing of labour:	68
On their own manual labour:	118
Not specified:	60

Fairs for livestock and pedlary were held on the first Friday (OS) in February, June 9th, August 17th and November 12th. A Manorial Court was held on the first Tuesday in every month.

One cannot write about Killough without mentioning the famous Scordon Waters. St Scordon's Well, noted for its extremely light water, was considered by many to have healing properties. There was also a mineral well situated near to the Charter School, which was said to be "purgative and emetic".

Both these water sources attracted visitors, looking for a cure, to Killough.

During the mid-eighteen hundreds Lord Bangor had a large reservoir constructed at considerable expense, to receive the constant flow of the water from Scordon. The water was then piped through the village. Fountains were conveniently placed to cater for the cottage dwellers and pipes connected to the principal houses, thus providing all the inhabitants with a constant supply of clean, fresh water. Compared with other villages of this time, Killough was fortunate indeed.

Another remarkable feature of Killough is the unusual oblong hole which can be found in the rocks beyond St. Scordon's Well (opposite to where the Coastguard Station is situated today). This strange sucking-hole of water which at high tide sends water spiralling up the narrow vent, making a noise resembling a hunting horn, is yet another of Killough's many attractions.

If we could travel back in time to when Killough was at its most prosperous, we would see a busy harbour, the hub of trade and industry; many fine houses owned by manufacturers and professional gentlemen; the Parish Church, whose wooden spire was a guide to mariners; the fine Parochial House in Castle Street with its porticos and stone urns; an impressive warehouse with its triple arch shop windows; a charming Wesleyan Methodist Preaching House with Gothic windows; the Coastguard Station with its turrets and boiling-oil hole windows; St Joseph's Catholic Chapel, built in 1828 and converted to a more attractive edifice in 1884; an octagonal windmill and stores (possibly a working mill at this time). There were also many large grain and coal stores, several small grocery shops, shoemaker and cobblers shops, a tailor and blacksmith's forges. The Scutch Mill and bleaching houses were places of industry, with the linen stretched out on the bleach greens. There was an R.I.C. Barracks in The Square, schools at either end of the village and a multitude of small dwellings following the curve of the bay.

To return for a moment to the Parish Church and its spire. This spire was blown down and the church roof severely damaged on the night of 'The Big Wind', January 12th.1839. An account of the damage was reported in the Down Recorder:

KILLOUGH - The storm on Sunday night, visited Killough with peculiar severity, as it must have done in all places of exposed situation. In the expressive language of some of the weather beaten veterans of that ancient harbour, the land breeze, that as it were, filled the streets with an irresistible flood of wind, was not a storm such as usually experienced in the severest weather, but a species of hurricane sweeping across the face of heaven, searching every corner and alley and scattering abroad everything that was found weak in itself and without firm support. No life has been lost here, but several houses have been unroofed, hovels blown to atoms, and the streets, in the morning, presented a huge mass of intermingled slates and thatch, on which were seen creeping a few isolated beings, driven out of their shelter at this inclement season. I am sorry to have to add, the pretty spire of the church, whose regular slating attracted the notice and praise of every observer, yielded to the fury of the elements and in its fall bent down the roof of the church, leaving its vertix in the very reading desk. I trust that something may be done by the Government to alleviate the sufferings of the wretches who are left destitute of shelter at this season.'

On the outskirts of the village stands an extensive and remarkably well laid out series of almshouses, known locally as 'The Institution'. These fine, stone dwellings are complimented by a bell tower. The almshouses were built at the bequest of Charles Sheils, a native of Killough. Charles Sheils left Killough as a young man to serve an apprenticeship in a mercantile establishment in London. He eventually became an assistant to an eminent Liverpool firm in the cotton trade. Good at his job he became a leading merchant and was made a partner of the company. He acquired a large fortune and married a girl from Tyrone. Sadly they had no children. When his fortune was made he returned to Ireland to reside in Killiney, Dublin.

For many years he donated the sum of £150 per annum to the deserving poor of Killough. Always deeply concerned with Irish Distress he set up soup

Captain Charles Walsh of Killough

Ellen Walsh (nee Ward) wife of Captain Charles Walsh

burial plot in the cemetery at St Anne's Church.

He bequeathed his entire fortune for the relief of distress in Ireland. He established almshouses in five different counties; Killough in Down, Carrickfergus in Antrim, Dungannon in Tyrone and Armagh and Dublin. His estate amounted to somewhere in the region of £100 000, and a detailed will outlined how the moneys were to be distributed and used for the upkeep of the almshouses.

It would appear that many who resided in the almshouses were distressed gentlefolk, not paupers. To avail oneself of the charity, a person had to be able to provide money for food and furnishings. When Ellen Walsh, wife of Captain Charles Walsh, a sea captain of Killough, was left a widow with three young sons, Gerard, Henry and Willie, she had to prove an income large enough to buy food and fuel before she was granted accommodation.

A true son of Killough, Charles Sheils is worthy of this epitaph:

> *He who hath pity on the poor,*
> *Lendeth to the Lord;*
> *And that which he hath given,*
> *He will repay him again.*

Proverbs 10-17

kitchens in Killough during the famine years and encouraged other wealthy inhabitants of the village to contribute towards feeding the poor. In the winter of 1847, the weather being bad, the fishermen of the village were unable to put to sea and their families suffered hardship. Charles Sheils organised relief by providing soup, free to those with no means of support, or at half a penny per quart.

In December 1861 Charles Sheils died in Killiney, Dublin. His remains were brought to Belfast by train then conveyed by hearse to his native town, Killough, for interment in the family

Another noteworthy figure born in Killough was Charles William Russell, who became the President of Maynooth in 1857 and held the post until his death in 1880. Charles William was the son of Charles Russell, a descendent of the Russell family who were given the lands of Killough after the Anglo-Norman invasion. Charles Russell came to Killough from Ballystrew in 1790 to set himself up as a merchant. He became a very wealthy man,

KILLOUGH REGATTA

WILL BE HELD

On MONDAY, 3rd JULY, 1893.

PATRONS:

Viscount Bangor
Lieut-Genl Lord de Ros
Major-General Browne
Lieut-Colonel Gracey

The Hon S Ward
E G Henesey, Esq, J P
C R Kelly, Esq, J P
T Andrews, Esq, J P

John Tate, Esq, J P
John Hutton, Esq, J P
B N Johnson, Esq
Wm Russell, Esq

COMMODORE:
The Right Hon Viscount Bangor.

VICE-COMMODORE:
C R Kelly, Esq, J P

COMMITTEE:

Dr Parkinson-Cumine
Captain Nelson
Mr N Hunter
„ F Murphy
„ John Montgomery
„ P Smith

Mr J Murphy
„ Joseph Carson
„ R Martin
„ P M'Lean
„ William Hughes
Captain W Burton

Captain James Burns
„ Thomas Hinds
Mr Robert Nelson
„ Geo Montgomery
„ A Munce

FIRST SAILING RACE, to start at 11-30 a.m.

Open to all Boats over 20ft., and not exceeding 30ft. over all. First Prize, £4; Second Prize, £1 10s; Third Prize, 10s. Time allowance, 20 seconds to the foot. Entrance, 2s 6d.

SECOND SAILING RACE, to start at Noon.

Open to all Boats not exceeding 20ft. over all. First Prize, £3; Second Prize, £1; Third Prize, 10s. Time allowance, 20 seconds to the foot. Entrance, 2s.

THIRD SAILING RACE, to start at 12-30 p.m.

Open to all Fishing Skiffs not exceeding 24ft. over all. First Prize, £2; Second Prize, £1; Third Prize, 10s. Time allowance, 20 seconds to the foot. Entrance, 1s.

FIRST ROWING RACE, to start at 2 p.m.

Open to all Four-oared Boats (Outriggers excepted.) First Prize, £2; Second Prize, £1; Third Prize, 10s. Entrance, 1s.

SECOND ROWING RACE, to start at 2-30 p.m.

Open to all Two-oared Boats (Outriggers excepted.) First Prize, £1; Second Prize, 10s, Third Prize, 5s. Entrance, 1s.

SCULLING RACE, to start at 3 p.m.

First Prize, £1; Second Prize, 10s; Third Prize, 5s. Entrance, 1s 6d.

A TEN-MILE BICYCLE ROAD RACE (Handicap), limited to a radius of fifteen miles, to start at 5 p.m. First Prize, Gold Medal, value £3; Second and Third Prizes, Silver Medals. Entrance, 1s 6d.

DUCK HUNT and other AQUATIC SPORTS. MAN RACES, GREASY POLE, &c.

REGULATIONS.

No Second Prize will be given in Sailing Races unless three Boats start, and no Third Prize unless five start. In case of a sail over only half value of First Prize will be given.

Entries for Sailing Races to be made on or before 6 p.m. on Saturday, 1st July.

In Rowing Races, no race unless two Boats start; no Second Prize unless three Boats start; and no Third Prize unless five Boats start and go the course.

Entries for Rowing Races received up to 10 a.m. on day of Races.

Entries for Bicycle Race to be made with Secretary before 4 o'clock on 30th June, with usual particulars.

The decision of the Committee to be final in all cases of dispute, without any appeal to a court of law, on which terms only will the Entries be received; and the Committee reserve the right to refuse any Entry or alter this programme if necessary.

A BAND WILL ATTEND.

G. M. SWAIL,
W. BURNS, } Hon. Secs.

H. FINLAY, Hon. Treasurer.

Killough Regatta poster, 1893

bought his own shop and built a fine house in Quay Lane, Killough.

In 1799 he married Anne McEvoy from Drogheda. She too came from a wealthy mercantile family. They had nine children, Charles William being the second youngest boy. The family were sufficiently wealthy to hire a private tutor for their sons and after receiving an elementary education at home, Charles William was enrolled as a pupil at Drogheda Grammar School. He lived with an aunt whilst he attended this school. He later transferred to Dr. Neilson's school in Downpatrick. This was a classical school which specialised in teaching Latin and Greek and had an excellent reputation. After two years at this school he was accepted at Maynooth. He was ordained a priest in 1835 and spent the rest of his life serving God.

When the grain trade collapsed many wealthy merchant families, like the Russells, found themselves in difficulties. The once busy harbour gradually grew still. One by one the grain stores closed and were left to fall into ruin.

People drifted away from the town and as the population diminished so did its prosperity. Failure to maintain the harbour and the upgrading of other local harbours stole away the fishing fleet and Belfast became the major port for merchant ships. The linen trade was overtaken by the cotton trade, as the latter was so much cheaper to produce. No longer one of the busiest ports in Lecale, Killough became the sleepy, fishing village that we know today.

The history so far recorded is beyond living memory. The next few paragraphs attempt to give an account of events within living memory.

Killough Brick Works Lorry, Henry Walsh at front

In the year 1900 Lord Bangor provided a cycle track on Castle Park, just beyond the Coastguard Station. For many years the local people made great use of this amenity. Belfast Ulster Directory (1900) comments:

"Children and friends can spend an enjoyable and profitable day, without any fear for their safety. No pleasanter resting place when mind and body are weary."

Sport was to the forefront of recreational activities in village life, football cricket and water sports all took place up at The Park.

The principal hotel at this time was called the 'Bangor Arms', now known as The Old Inn. It is said that it was a remarkably clean hotel, the tariff moderate and every attention paid to the visitor. The public houses too were known by different names.

The Saddle or Sail was called the 'Park Hotel' and McKeating's Anchor Bar was the 'Anchor Hotel'. Being near to the railway station the Ann Boal Inn was called the 'Railway Hotel'.

The brick works at Strand End in Killough was founded by McGladdery of Belfast in 1913. It was for many years one of the principal brick producing companies in Northern Ireland. It has been closed and re-opened several times during the past few decades. It is now called Strangford Brick and is currently in production (1990).

World War II temporarily increased the population of the village as evacuees from Belfast poured into Killough. Belfast was a prime target for bombing by German aircraft, so many of its citizens escaped to the relative peace and safety of Killough. They were still very much aware that there was a war going on because the bombers passed over the village at night, carrying their deadly cargo to

Railway Station, Killough

Belfast. The bombers would line themselves up with the Water Rock and then head for Belfast. On their return they would fly out over the lighthouse at St. John's Point. Many evacuees would watch the comings and goings of these aeroplanes and wonder about the safety of their friends and relatives back home in Belfast. Food was plentiful in Killough. There were home-grown vegetables, eggs and butter. In Belfast rationing was very strict and black market prices high. The Belfast refugees would send food to their families in Belfast to comfort them in their hardship.

English and American troops were also stationed in Killough. They were billeted under canvass at nearby St John's Point and the various halls in the village. The Scutch Mill, Edgehill, Kinvara and the large house attached to the Post Office all provided accommodation for the troops. Kinvara was the Officers' Mess and where the Courtyard is now was the Sergeants' Mess. St. Joseph's Hall, the Hibernian Hall and a coal store on the harbour were used as canteens or billets. Many of the local girls worked in the NAAFI at St John's Point whilst others gathered in the Rectory to knit comforts for servicemen abroad. Some of the girls did laundry for the troops. The soldiers practiced firing from the harbour wall and there was a whole battery of anti-aircraft guns at St John's Point which made the most horrific noise when they were fired. Two of the best remembered British Regiments stationed in Killough were the Royal Artillery and the Welch Fusiliers.

The railway line from Downpatrick, opened in 1892, provided a vital link with the county town and the city of Belfast. The railway station saw many arrivals and departures that are a part of the village history. Unfortunately the branch line closed in 1952 but there are hopes that it will re-open in the future.

The past four decades have seen an increase in the number of houses in Killough. The Northern Ireland Housing Executive has erected a variety of dwellings in the village. Most recently they have built a number of houses in Main Street which are very much in character with the village. A private development of bungalows in School Road and Church View, built by Burns & Co., add a pleasing dimension, being attractive in design and tastefully laid out.

Recently the most discussed topic in the village is the proposal to build a Marina. The Department for the Environment has given its approval in principle for the construction of a 300-berth yacht facility in the harbour of Killough. The Marina plan is opposed by conservationists, who are concerned about the wildlife in the Bay, and the residents of the tiny community of Coney Island who have raised objection to the suggestion that silt, from the harbour mouth, may be dumped on their shores. No development has yet taken place but the quaint, stone bridge at Strand End Lough, where the kingfishers previously nested, has been replaced by a concrete monstrosity to prevent the flooding of neighbouring farm land.

This is part of the history of Killough, over one thousand years of change. Change it may, survive and flourish it will, because Killough now has a community which cares. They will ensure its place in history.

Naming the Names

Every village has familiar surnames that have been in use for hundreds of years. In Killough these names are Russell, Ranaghan, McIlmale, Nelson, McCormick, Fitzsimons, Starkey and many more. These names appear in documents that record the history of the village. Some of these names have been in use in this area for almost a thousand years, the ancestors of these families coming to Ireland with John De Courcy at the time of the Anglo-Norman Invasion.

Talking about these old family names to Gerard Walsh inspired him to compile a list of the names of many of the families who lived in the village when he was a boy. Gerard is the oldest living Killough born and reared inhabitant of the village today. Born in 1905, Gerard has seen many changes in Killough. His brother, Henry, younger by two years could also recall many of the names, some no longer in use in the village, the families having gone away or died without issue.

The names of the roads and streets have also changed with time and so, as you read Gerard and Henry's list you discover yet another facet of the history of Killough.

Castle Street, circa 1950

EARLY KILLOUGH FAMILIES
BASED ON A RENTAL OF 1748 (PRONI D2092/1/7/1)

	Rent £
Samuel Moore	11.14. 1%
Patrick Fitzsimmons	1.10.0
Henry and widow Fitzsimmons	2.10.0
Samuel Brown	1.10.0
James Parkinson and Nick Killen's holding	0.10.0
Thomas Henry	3.0.0
Bryan Lenethy for Wm Fitzsimmons	1.0.0
James Fitzsimmons shoemaker	3.0.0
Mrs Mary Brett	9.0.0
James Portor's executors	3.5.0
James Tumulty for Nick Fitzsimmons	3.10.0
William Brett	12.12.0
The heirs of Richard Caddell	3.0.0
Mr Charles Hamilton now Robert Quaile	3.14.0
Mrs Lascelles for all her holdings	7.7.0
Mr James Feattus	13.0.0
Robert Ward Esq	3.0.0
Robert Quaile	1.10.0
Andrew Pringle	1.13.4
John Johnston	1.10.0
Henry Mulhollam	3.0.0
James Savage	6.0.0
Joseph McCullagh	1.5.0
James Moorehead	1.10.0
Captain Henry Crawford	44.3.8
Robert Kelly	3.0.0
The heirs of William Montgomery Esq	3.0.0
John Smith	1.10.10
Nathaniel Carson	1.10.0
Thomas Durkey	0.10.10
William Fitzpatrick	1.10.10
Nicholas Dornon	2.10.0
Thomas Dizney for Mackineys holding	1.10.0
Salt works Thomas Maxwell	4.10.0
The executors of Mr William Dizney	19.2.1 %
John Holland	0.8.9
James Cargey	0.15.0
Alexander O'Dair	1.10.0
Mr Robert Smith	1.10.0
Thomas Parkinson Exors	6.0.0
Michael Seeds	3.10.0
Mr Nicholas Pine	1.10.0
William Mullan	1.10.0
Mr Thomas Bourton	1.10.0
James Clerk	7.0.0
Thomas Maxwell	0.10.0
John Biggan	0.10.0
John Cottor	2.0.0
Widow Walsh	0.5.0
Windmill - Cargey and McCullough	23.0.0
Marle Bogg Ballyligg tenants	1.5.0
Executors Mt William Bizney Bleachyard	2.14.0
Mr Hall. Clover field etc.	6.4.10%
Richard Cane Fishers park	2.8.9
Thiep? Ranaghan	6.0.0
Bryan McClean, tenant set Novr 1751	
Daniel Dogherty Do.	
Patrick Mulhollam Do.	
James Maxwell Do.	
Hugh Donaghey sett Novr 1748	
Patrick Burns Do	

POINT ROAD

Blythe (bookmaker)
Taylor

BARRACK'S LANE (CHAPEL LANE)

Rose Kane (grew and sold herbs)	McClean
Smyth	McIlmail
McMullan	Milligan
Taylor	Taylor
McCullough	Sloan
Hanna	Duffy (tailor)
Deegan	Ward
Connolly	Murphy

MAIN STREET (CASTLE STREET) (LEFT)

Annie Dougan (shopkeeper)	McSherry (fisherman)
Evans	McKermitt (labourer)
Savage (publican)	Fitzsimons
Smyth (shopkeeper)	McSherry (farmworker)
Dagens	McIhone
Denis Waterson (publican)	Hunter (shopkeeper)
Denvir	Davidson (farmer)
Gardener	Mageen
Connolly	McCormick (blacksmith)
Russell Kelly (merchant)	Walsh (seaman)
Gartland (midwife)	Nelson (farmer)
Denvir	Hanna (shopkeeper)

GERARD AND HENRY'S LISTS

FISHERMAN'S ROW

Armstrong	McAllister
Hinds	Green
James	Small - up Elbow Lane
McGonigle	Fitzsimons
Coffey	Morgan
Briggs	Keown
McSherry	Teer
Donnan	Doran
Burns	McIlmail
Parkinson	Smyth
Simmons	Bob Steele
Jordan	Cargill (shoemaker)

PALATINE LANE

Caher
Dagens
Torney (lodging House)
Cochrane
West
Ritchie

PALATINE SQUARE

Ranaghan (farmer)
Dr McComiskey (GP)
Despard (Captain)

CARMAN'S ROW (MAIN STREET)

McConvey (farmer)
Blayney
Mulvenna (shoemaker)
Smith
Murphy (publican)
McCance (builder/shopkeeper)
Burke
Smalls
Walls / Irvine
McClure (blacksmith)

McGinn
Craig
Sharvin
McClean
Davidson
McMurray (shopkeeper)
Connolly (car man)
Montgomery (Post Office)
Kenney
Flanaghan

QUAY LANE

Burton (publican)
Bell
McGreevy (butcher)
Ward
O'Prey
Ward
McCormick

MAIN STREET (CASTLE STREET) (RIGHT)

Buckley (schoolmaster)
Ryans (policeman/railway guard)
Parkinson (GP)
Keating (lighthouse keeper)
McMaster
Nelson (farmer)
O'Prey (sailor)
O'Brien (army sergeant/sea captain)
Fagen

Burns (schoolmaster)
Finlay (Lord Bangor's Agent)
Murphy (shopkeeper)
Starkey (sea captain)
Munce
McClean (sea captain)
Branney (car man)
Denvir (teacher)
McIlmail

Gerard also compiled a list of Sea Captains from Killough. This could be something of a record for so many Captains to come from one small village. The list covers the last century, the captains being either deep sea or coastal seamen.

Captain Nelson
Captain Cotter
Captain McClean (there were 3 captains bearing this name)
Captain Denvir (there were 2 captains bearing this name)
Captain Crangle (there were 4 captains bearing this name)
Captain Charles Walsh (Gerard, Henry and William Walsh's father)
Captain Starkey
Captain Killen

Captain Munce
Captain O'Brien
Captain Hicks
Captain Burton
Captain Vaughan
Captain Hinds
Captain Finlay
Captain Adair

For those of you interested in matters of the sea, here is a list of arrivals and sailings, in and out of Killough harbour in October, 1845. This list covers only five days in October and proves what a busy port Killough must have then been.

ARRIVALS

Ship type & name	Name of Master	Home Port	Cargo	From
Sloop, Jane	P Corran	Killough	coals	Whitehaven
Sloop, Brothers	A Hill	Killough	coals	Whitehaven
Smack, Venus	Kelly	Castletown	coals	Troon
Sloop, Hannah & Mary	J Hill	Killough	coals	Whitehaven
Sloop, Roberts	McSherry	Killough	coals	Whitehaven
Smack, Dasher	McCartan	Killough	coals	Liverpool
Schooner, Don Juan	Gilpin	Dundalk		Troon
Schooner, St Michael	Hinds	Killough	flour	Dundalk
Schooner, Betty	Killen	Killough	coals	Liverpool
Schooner, Swallow	Boyd	Newry	coals	Whitehaven
Smack, Eliza	Starkey	Killough	bones & rags	Newry

SAILINGS	*To*
Schooner, Countess	Maryport
Smack, Venus	Dundalk
Schooner, Don Juan	Dundalk

From this list it can be derived that boats from the South of Ireland used Killough as a stopping off place en route from Troon to their home port. The boats usually stayed two days in Killough. The primary cargo for Killough boats appears to have been coals, mostly from Whitehaven in Cumbria. On 7th October alone, 150 tons of coal was transported from Killough quay to users in the area. Coal from Whitehaven fetched 16 shillings per ton, while coal from Liverpool fetched only 14 shillings per ton.

Killough Bay and its surrounding headlands have been witness to the inevitable tragedies that take place at sea. Down through the ages seamen have battled against the elements and many fine ships and precious lives have been lost. This list records some of the major tragedies that took place in the waters along our coastline.

1796   The 'Hope', a cargo ship, ran aground near Killough

1830   The 'Dale' of Maryport was lost with all hands on board near Killough

1836   On 16th December the Schooner 'Minapia' foundered off St John's Point. All hands were lost. In St Anne's Churchyard, where the crew of the 'Minapia' are buried, the inscription on the headstone reads:

Here lies the bodies of Killaly William Musgrave aged 19 and Aran Bellingham aged 27 years, mate, son and son-in-law of the late William Musgrave, civil engineer to the Port and Harbour of the city of Waterford, together with the captain and the rest of the crew of that ill-fated vessel, the Minapia of Waterford, which was lost on the rocks off St John's Point on the night of the 13th December 1836, not one surviving to tell the melancholy tale.

Captain Charles Walsh and the crew of SS Barshaw

1854   2nd July. It was a foggy morning when the brig 'Nova Providenza' ended her days. She finished up on the rocks at Ringfad Point. Much to the delight of the villagers her wreck was sold by auction, providing firewood and fencing for the village for some time.

1856   5th April. The 'Nautilus', a smack owned by Thomas Russell sank near Killough

1918   21st Oct. 'Saint Barchan' was lost when she was torpedoed off Killough by a U-Boat. Eight merchant seamen lost their lives, the last to do so in home waters.

1844 The lighthouse at St John's Point was erected, a shining beacon, guiding the sailor safely on his way. The fishermen of Ardglass today say that they are always glad to see St John's Light. They know that they are nearly home and that the light will make their passage safe.

At the turn of the century the lighthouse was raised two floors. The light was gas-powered and the gas was made at the Point. Three light-keepers and their families lived in the houses at the foot of the lighthouse. After the First World War incandescent paraffin was used to power the light. In 1954 the lighthouse exterior was extensively renovated and in 1980 the light was electrified. This reduced the need for three light-keepers down to one. The lighthouse keeper today (May 1990) is Harry Henvey, who, along with his wife Mary, lives under the towering height, the sole keeper of St John's Light.

Street Names in Killough

Many of the streets are named after a particular building to be found in the street. For example, Chapel Lane leads to St Joseph's Roman Catholic Church. School Road is so called because there used to be a National School at the end of the road nearest to the Chapel. Prior to being called School Road it was known as Mill Road because of the windmill at the rear of the road. Fisherman's Row was obviously christened so because the small cottages were more than likely inhabited by fishermen and their families. The Point Road leads to St John's Point, and the Rossglass Road naturally goes to Rossglass. Castle Street, named possibly for the castle-like structure on the harbour, was once called Main Street. Main Street was previously called Carman's Row because a number of jaunting car and carriage men lived there.

Perhaps the most unusual street name is the one given to Palatine Lane and the Square. They were named after a group of refugees from Palatine, a German Province, in the 17th Century. After some religious persecution these people fled their country and were granted provision by the Irish Parliament in 1709 to settle in Ireland. The Palatines split into two factions. One group stayed here in Killough, they were employed in the linen industry, the others went to Limerick, they were lace-makers.

The Ropewalk was used in the days of sailing ships for stretching out the long ropes and Elbow Lane is shaped like your elbow. Newer additions to the list of names are those of Kennedy Park and Church View, the former being named in honour of the late John F Kennedy. Station Road will always remind us of the days when the train came to Killough.

Date List

This list of dates may help in placing some of the events that have been mentioned in this book but not dated.

1716 St Anne's Parish Church, rebuilt on the foreshore in the form that it is today.

1724 Salt works constructed.

1733 The Charter School opened.

1781 Ward family elevated to the Peerage.

1812 St Anne's Church required some rebuilding.

1826	Wesleyan Church constructed (now Clinic).
1827	Alexander Nimmo commissioned by Lord Bangor, 3rd Viscount, to build the harbour.
1828	St Joseph's Catholic Church built. Money for the building was mainly provided by a merchant called Rogan. Prior to the church being built mass was said at a Mass Rock near Coniamstown. The Parish Priest at the time was Rev Father Richard McMullan. It was consecrated by Dr Crolley.
1839	The Great Wind. Spire blown from St Anne's Church, and sails blown from windmill.
1844	The establishment of a lighthouse at St John's Point.
1844	St Joseph's Catholic Church altered.
1850	The sycamore trees were planted in the main thoroughfare, once known as Main Street, now called Castle Street.
1886	Sheils Institution built at bequest of Charles Sheils.
1892	Railway line from Downpatrick to Killough and Ardglass opened.
1913	New brickworks opened.
1943	The last coal boat sailed into Killough Harbour.
1950	The railway line from Downpatrick to Killough and Ardglass closed.
1960	Harbour Improvement Committee formed.
1964	Village Committee formed.
1970	Down District Council took the harbour into Public Ownership.
1981	The village was declared a Conservation area.
1982	Vesting order under Local Government Act of 1922 and Harbour Act of 1910.
1983	Restoration work on the Pier begins. Support from EEC.
1988	Public Enquiry.
1989	Go ahead for the Marina.

Messenger boy from Hunter's stores

Every Village has its Story

Every village has its own stories and tales and Killough is no exception. When we set out to collect the stories, we approached the senior citizens of the village. Before long we discovered a wealth of legends, historical anecdotes, place-names no longer in use, recollections of occupations and leisure pursuits that are no longer followed, school days and a treasure trove of funny tales. These are the memories of old Killough, a part of the history of the people of our village.

We have recorded them just as they were told. There are no exact times, locations or names attached to many of the stories and that they are not told in any particular order neither detracts nor diminishes their value, as each story stands in its own right. These are tales that are worth telling again and again.

These are the stories that our storytellers referred to as "good value". As the tales were recalled and memories rekindled we often heard the phrases "Ah, but it's all changed now" and "Those were the days".

"What fun we had on a warm, summer Saturday night and what energy we used up, swapping all the summer seats that sat outside the houses in Castle Street and Main Street. We took the seat from the first house to the last house and so on, all undercover of darkness. Sunday morning, you should have seen their faces, as front doors were opened by early morning Mass goers. That is, those that could still open their doors. Them that couldn't had a summer seat tied to the door handle and they were trapped until someone came to let them out."

"Talking of people trapped in doors, did you hear the one about the 'ould fella' who didn't come out for three days? Well, it goes like this and the boys responsible, each one an 'ould fella' himself now, still living in Killough. We found some black paint and decided to paint the windows of this man's house, the glass that is not the frames. We gave each pane a real good coating, so that every time the old man got out of bed and drew back his curtains it was always dark. So he hopped back into bed to wait for the morning. It was only when the neighbours got worried, having not seen him about, that somebody went and got him up out of bed. Otherwise he could have been there yet."

"Many of our biggest laughs were at someone else's expense but for most they were taken in good part. The ones who had their chimneys bagged only coughed for a short while. It was good sport, you know, to climb up on the low roof of a house and 'bag the chimney' with a wet sack. The smoke would come billowing down the chimney, blackening everything and everybody in the house. We would hang about outside, waiting for them to come hurtling through the door, coughing and spluttering, their eyes streaming as they hurled curses at us for tormenting them so."

"Bagging a chimney was a great way of getting your revenge if you hadn't been invited into a house to join in the fun. One night we bagged a chimney on Fisherman's Row. They were all inside enjoying a tasty chips and peas supper, brought in from John Mitchell's Chip Shop, and we were left outside. So, up on the roof we went and carried out an old trick. Not long after that somebody painted a sign on a wall close by the house that read 'Bill's Buffet', with an arrow pointing to the house where the supper eaters had come to a sooty end."

"We were always writing signs to get a laugh at

somebody. Who was it who wrote 'BLACK BALLS 4d A QUARTER STONE' on the Battery Wall, opposite the house of a certain gentleman who bought a bag of these black balls from Teague's Shop every day? I don't remember now."

If some details have slipped the memory it is only to be expected, but for everyone forgotten a hundred were remembered. And so the stories continue.

MARRIED OUT OF PITY, THEN FOR LOVE AND FINALLY FOR CHARITY

Thomas Teer was a tailor and a Methodist preacher here in Killough. He was engaged to Barbara Meredith, a girl from Strangford. Whilst attending a Methodist Conference he met Fanny Glover. He was overcome with compassion for her. (She may have been a little on the plain side, we think). He told Barbara he was going to marry Fanny out of pity. Fanny had two daughters to Thomas before she died. Thomas then married Barbara, for love, she had three daughters. After Barbara's death Thomas needed someone to look after his family so he craftily married his housekeeper, Cynthia Park of Ardglass. And so it was said "Thomas Teer who married out of pity then for love and finally for charity".

Shortly after her marriage to Thomas, Cynthia met a countrywoman, Kate McCready, whilst out shopping.

"Morning, Miss Park," greeted Kate.
"I'm married now," Cynthia replied.
To which Kate enquired, "Oh! Who did you get?"
Proudly Cynthia told her, "Thomas Teer, a son of God"

Quickly Kate retorted, "Well, tell him from me, he'll never see his father".

Thomas Teer had a preaching house which was at the rear of what is now Duffy's shop. The choirmaster was Joseph Surch. During choir practices he would place an upright penny between the teeth of the singers, to make sure their mouths would open wide enough to let the sound come out.

Cynthia (the charity wife) outlived Thomas, who died at the early age of forty-six years. "It was just as well he died young," remarked a neighbour, "For had he lived to be an old man he would have been as bad as Solomon". Charitably, Cynthia buried him beside his second wife, Barbara (married for love).

ONE SWALLOW DOESN'T MAKE A SUMMER

A family called Swallow came from Downpatrick to Killough each summer for their holidays. Villagers would say: "The good weather is here for the Swallow's have arrived".

BLOOMERS

Woe betide any lazy housewife in Killough who neglected to bring in her washing. There were boys in the village who crept into the gardens at night, tied knots in the legs of the bloomers and filled them with stones.

ASS BY THE HEARTH

A very deaf old woman called Mary lived in a house on Fisherman's Row.

The cottage had a narrow, half-leaf door. One evening whilst she was out at the back of the house the boys decided to play a trick on her. Near the house stood a donkey and cart. First they

Methodist Meeting House, Main Street, circa 1890

unharnessed the donkey, next they took the wheels off the cart. Then they tipped the cart on its side and pushed it through the narrow doorway. Rolling the wheels in, they uprighted the cart in front of the fireplace in the tiny living room. They fastened the wheels back on and then brought in the donkey. When the donkey was placed between the shafts his head was almost up the chimney.

When the poor old dear returned indoors she just couldn't understand how the donkey and cart had managed to squeeze through the narrow door. She ran outside to tell her neighbours about her unexpected visitor. They too were mystified as to how the beast had got through the door. Then along came 'the boys'.

Mary, by this time, was in a panic. How was she going to get the animal out of her kitchen? She wanted to know. Naturally, 'the boys' had the solution. In they went and brought out the donkey and cart in much the same manner as they had put it in. Mary was impressed with this bit of clever thinking and told them they were "smart lads". Had she known the whole story it is doubtful she would have still held that opinion.

THE EFFERVESCING PO

In a house at the corner of Chapel Lane lived a man called Paddy O'Reilly. Paddy was very interested in football. The young men of the village would meet in Paddy's house to talk about the game. 'Ma' O'Reilly, who always wore a griddle hat, was usually present at these meetings. Being rather whiskery about the chin, she reminded the boys of a nanny goat. They would 'Baa-aa' when they were talking to her, to which she would growl, "Ach, away out o' that". One young fellow, a regular visitor to the house, noticed that Mrs O' Reilly had a routine carried out each time he and the others were present. She would make tea for them, then she would bid them goodnight, go through to the scullery and return with the chamber pot which she always took with her into the bedroom, to use before retiring for the night.

So, one night, whilst Mrs O'Reilly drank her tea with the rest of them, this young fellow excused himself and left the room, indicating he was going "out to the yard". He slipped into the scullery and emptied the entire contents of a tin of Andrew's Liver Salts into the chamber pot. He had taken the tin from his father's shop (Now do you know who he is?). As usual, Mrs O'Reilly finished her tea, got the chamber pot and went into the bedroom. There was an almighty yell as the poor woman filled the pot and the Liver Salts frothed up to the brim.

Group at lime kiln circa 1900

NEVER PLAY CARDS WITH A STRANGER

One stormy, wintry night there was a knock on the door of a house of a woman who lived alone. It was a tall, dark stranger asking for shelter. To pass the evening they played cards. During a game the woman dropped a card on the floor. When she stooped to pick it up she saw a cloven hoof and realised who her visitor was. She fled from the house towards the churchyard, as the Devil is supposed to have no power on consecrated ground. Sadly, she never reached the churchyard and as the Devil caught her he cried, "Mine, Mine, Mine".

Bus to Downpatrick for replay of North Down Championship, Killough v Ballyculter, 1934

LESLIE'S LONEY

Up St John's Point Road there is a laneway called Leslie's Loney, which got its name from a man who lived there a long time ago. He was a notorious card player. One night, after playing cards at the usual haunt, he left to go home and was never seen again. Legend has it that he met the Devil who challenged him to a game of cards for his soul. The Devil won the game. A more likely conclusion is that Leslie slipped away on one of the bigger boats that used to put into Killough, leaving his debts behind him.

BILLY PORTER'S LINK

In 1882 a family named Porter lived at the southern end of Leslie's Loney. At this time the news was gathered and distributed by visiting different houses in the district. The kettle would be put on the fire and, if the news was interesting, a hot drink would be given to the visitor. (A hot drink could have been boiling water poured over blackcurrant leaves, as tea cost twenty shillings a pound in those days). If the Porter's didn't find the news interesting enough to offer refreshment they raised the kettle higher on the crane. This happened so often at Porter's that "Billy Porter's link" became a common expression, if, when out visiting, you were not offered a cup of "tea".

THE JERUSALEM DONKEY

Before the age of motor cars the Killough Parish Priest was Father Brennan. One day when he was out driving in his pony and trap, down the Quarter Hill, he met John Perry with his donkey and cart. John was beating the donkey unmercifully. "John!" the Priest remonstrated, "You should not beat a donkey like that. Our Lord rode into Jerusalem on an ass".

"Well Father," John replied, "If it was this one He wouldn't have been there yet".

ADAM'S HOLE

One morning, like most mornings, Adam Chapman loaded up his cart with fish to sell around the countryside. As he was harnessing the donkey to the cart out came his wife, guldering at him as usual. "Don't you bother to come home until you've sold every bit of that fish," she said, threateningly.

Miserably, Adam set out on his rounds. Business that day was not good, and by evening Adam still had quite a bit of fish left over. Rather than face his targe of a wife he came to a dreadful decision. On reaching a large clay hole, filled with water, on the Killough Road near the brick works, he stopped. He stuffed all the money he had earned that day into the mouth of the largest remaining fish. Giving the donkey a slap he left it to find its own way home, then threw himself down the hole and drowned.

NELSON IN KILLOUGH

Nelson may have won the Battle of Trafalgar but he was less than victorious when he appeared in Killough. On seeing a picture of Killough Harbour in the Dublin Independent, the local boys were more than annoyed because the newspaper had superimposed a picture of Nelson on the harbour. "What the F... has Nelson to do with Killough?" the lads grumbled. It was then that they decided to make an effigy of that famous admiral. They dressed him in an old frock coat and breeches. They stuck a feather in his hat, a bottle in his pocket, and hung a sword from his belt. Who the breeches belonged to we do not know but it was Jimmy Seed's sword.

When they had him finished they tied him up high in a tree, which stood near to where the car park is today. He hung there for quite a while, an object of ridicule to some. When the stone throwers got tired of him they decided to take him down and burn him. But just as they lowered him to the ground, the number 34 bus, going to Ardglass, arrived.

"Hey lads," shouted one of the fellows, "Lets send this bag o' shite to Ardglass." They threw him up on to the upper deck of the open-top bus, and that was the last time Admiral Nelson was seen in Killough.

RIVAL DITTIES

There was always great rivalry between Killough and Ardglass, particularly when they played football. A match, which took place at the time of the Dublin Congress, between the two towns ended in bitter fighting because Killough had won the game. Maybe there would have been a fight no matter which side had won.

They even had rival ditties. This is what Killough thought about Ardglass:

"Killough it is a nice wee place
It's all surrounded by trees.
But when you go to Ardglass
You're clobbered up to the knees."

Ardglass would reply with:

"Killough it is a dirty old hole,
They burn the wrack to save the coal.
They gather whelks to save the milk,
And that is why they can all wear silk."

HARVEST TIME TALES

At harvest time in Killough it was usual for

everyone to pray for good weather, but one particular summer was extremely dry and the crops lay withering in the fields. Fearing the harvest would be a total disaster the Parish Priest at that time, Father McArdle, prayed from the altar for rain. The rains came and looked set to continue for some time. Those who had complained about the long, dry spell, now complained of the incessant rain. Father McArdle, feeling somewhat to blame for the continuing downpour, then asked a woman who prayed to St Anne to pray for the rain to stop. "No," replied the woman. "You asked for it from the altar, yourself, so now you're getting plenty of it."

When the harvest was being gathered it was the duty of the farmer's wife to provide food for the harvesters. After toiling in the fields all morning one young fellow sat down at the farmer's table and, picking up a slice of thick homemade bread, he buttered it on both sides. The farmer's wife, a bit taken aback by his extravagance, asked him why he had done this. "I've as good a taste on my bottom lip as I have on my top." he replied.

AGNEW'S GRAVE

A short distance from Killough, at the crossroads before Bright Church, is a place called Agnew's Grave. Here there lived a woman whose name was Agnew. She had a young son. One day she told the boy to look after some young chickens and to make sure no harm came to them while she went into town to do her messages. Trying to be helpful he placed a three-legged pot over them. When his mother returned she found the chickens to be smothered. Angrily, she hit the boy. He fell, hitting his head on a stone. The mother thought her child was unconscious and tried to revive him. To her horror she found that he was dead. Driven out of her mind with grief and remorse, she hanged herself. It was forbidden to bury the body of a suicide on consecrated ground and so she was laid to rest nearby.

Harvest Time: 1930's in Foy's Field at Sheils' Buildings.

From back row (l–r) Charles Foy, John Blayney, Willie Ross, Hugh Blayney, Willie Walsh, John McClean, Joseph Dagens

Front: Unknown (possibly Patsy Stewart

OVER THE RIVER

"Over the river, happy forever." This old sailors' saying applied to crossing the small river which runs down the side of Elbow Lane to the foot of Fisherman's Row before joining the sea. Further along Fisherman's Row we join the road that leads to St. Helena's Beach and Scordon. This sandy beach was called after an anchorite hermit who once lived there. Of Scordon's Bank there is this ditty:

"Dirty Ardglass and Dirty Ballyhornan,
But sweet Killough and the Bonny Bank of
Scordon."

MUG'S VILLAS

In summertime the nuns had bathing boxes at St Helena's Beach. The local people respected the nuns' privacy while they bathed. The nuns came to Killough every summer, often bringing with them deprived children from the city. The house in which they stayed was on the Point Road. It was one of the two houses known locally as Mug's Villas. These houses were built by William Blythe, who on his return from America, opened a betting shop in Belfast. While he was in Buffalo, USA, his wife gave birth to a daughter, Ethel. She married James Stewart of Stewart Motor Works, Downpatrick. At the end of World War II Ethel was commissioned,

Hunter's Store, circa 1900

with Lady Antrim, to go to Germany during the Liberation. Ethel was a trained nurse. Because she had retained her American passport she was the only person from Britain to enter Belsen concentration camp, in the rescue of those so cruelly imprisoned there.

Yet another story involving a member of the Stewart family. In August, 1921, the County Down Motorcycle Club held a race, the first of its kind, in Killough. The three-lap circuit was over 36 miles and contained many hairpin bends. This event was organised to coincide with a local sports meeting and had been postponed for a week, until 17th August, owing to bad weather. The weather was not much better when the race took place according to a report in the Irish Cyclist and Motor Cyclist. There were only four competitors but the event created great enthusiasm in the neighbourhood. All the hairpin bends were crowded with spectators,

also the start and finishing lines. The winner of the race was James Stewart, husband of Ethel, (mentioned in previous story) of Stewart's Motor Works, Downpatrick. He rode a Harley Davidson machine. James Stewart and his wife, Ethel, were the parents of Mr Jack Stewart who, at the present time, resides at the Point Road.

THE DISTRICT NURSE

In a house in Castle Street lived the local midwife, Nurse Gartland. She was a Scots woman. She rode about the countryside on a bicycle with her medical bag strapped to the carrier. She delivered Gerard Walsh, who, born and reared in Killough, is the oldest native at this time (April 1990). Gerard, a well-known character, is 85 years old. If Nurse Gartland was needed during the night someone had to collect her in a horse and cart. A meticulous and houseproud woman, she referred to cobwebs as "Irish Curtains".

On the Wall at Scordon 1936:
(l-r) T. Connolly, W. Ross,
G. Walsh, T. Taylor.

Bathing at the pier, circa 1910

ALONG THE BATTERY WALL

Long before modern day plumbing the houses in Killough had dry closets, the contents of which had to be emptied out on to the shore. One unfortunate chap, who happened to be walking beneath the Battery Wall, looked up just in time to get the contents of Mary's bucket, full in the face.

STRANNEY'S WALLS

Before you come to the Battery Wall there used to be three houses that were known as 'the Court'. There was a wall round these houses which was called Stranney's Walls, maybe after a family of that name. There was a water pump here. Anthony and Vincey Teague, two senior citizens, born and reared and still living in the village today, can remember collecting water by the bucketful from this pump for use in their own home. They were given a penny a week for this job. With the penny they were able to buy ten gobstoppers, the kind that changed colour as they were sucked.

SCHOOL DAYS

No longer can children avoid their school lessons by offering to clean out the stove in the classroom or sweep down the stairs, but Mary Ellen McIlmale

Waiting for the first train to arrive in Killough, 1892

can remember doing just that. Mary Ellen, or Mamie, as she is also known, is a bright, cheery senior citizen living in Killough, as she has done all her life. She recalls children walking to school in their bare feet. Many of these children came from the outlying farms and walked long distances. She laughs when she recalls how the pupils had to line up to go to the toilet. As they filed out and across the yard the teacher would watch them by standing on a ledge to look out of the classroom window. After the long queue had all paid their 'visits' he would rap sharply on the window to signal them back in again.

The children brought their own lunches in dinner pails, the contents of these pails often being eaten long before dinnertime. They also had to pay for their books and bring turf for the fire. The girls were taught cookery and laundry work. One day in the laundry class, a girl who had not been paying attentions was asked, "How do you hang out combinations?" The girl replied, "By the toe." and the class roared with laughter.

A favourite trick with all school children seems to have been for them to place drawing pins on the teacher's chair. The boys in Mr Buckley's school would do this regularly, in the days when Mary Ellen McIlmale was a pupil.

WILLIAM THE CONQUEROR

In a field up at the Point was a white horse that had never been ridden by any man. Try as they might the local boys, who went up to the Point for an afternoon's sport, could not ride the beast. It became such a challenge that fellows from miles around the countryside would gather on a Sunday afternoon in anticipation of seeing someone make the conquest. One such fellow was Willie Walsh of Killough. One bright summer day Willie mounted the horse and, to the astonishment of all the onlookers, rode triumphantly round the field. The Killough boys cheered for their champion who had managed to beat challengers from Rossglass, Ballynoe, Tyrella, etc. They dubbed Willie "The Conqueror", a name which stuck for the rest of his life. Little did the other challengers know that Willie had secretly been feeding the horse with titbits for several weeks. And we all know "you never bite the hand that feeds you." (Willie died in 1986, aged 76).

TWO LUCKY MEN

In the days when coal boats came into Killough Harbour there were several coal yards in the village. One of these belonged to Tommy McEvoy. He had inherited it from the publican, Francis Murphy. This yard was in Carman's Row. Another coal yard, owned by Reggie William, was in Quay Lane. As Jack Stewart told us. "These must have been two of the luckiest fellows in Killough because Tommy, who inherited the coal yard, was also left a farm of land by a childless couple. Reggie was left the ownership of Hunter's Stores by the Hunter's, who were also childless. Hunter's Stores is now Duffy's Shop."

LUKEY GRIBBON

When the horse and cart were still used to transport goods to and from the harbour a carrier, called Lukey Gribbon, met with a most unfortunate experience. Whilst he was trying to conveniently position the cartload of potatoes at the edge of the quay, he reversed the horse and cart just that little bit too much, so that load, cart, horse and Lukey plunged down, discharging his load in a most untimely manner.

SOMETHING FOR NOTHING

In a house in Main Street lived a man called Sean Collins. He used a paraffin stove to heat the house. Like all of us Sean liked something for nothing, so when a fellow he met out in the country one day offered to get him paraffin for nothing, Sean readily accepted. Later that week, on a cold night, Sean decided to light the stove. He lit it and as the fuel ignited the stove exploded blowing the roof off the house, leaving Sean, somewhat singed, staring up at the stars. It was only afterwards that Sean discovered his supplier worked at Bishopscourt, and the fuel was aviation fuel. Was this the first rocket propelled stove in Killough? And if so, would it have interested Rex McCandless?

REX MCCANDLESS

When acclaimed inventor Rex McCandless retired in the mid 1970s he chose to settle in Killough. He bought the old railway goods shed and a few acres of land. He created a lake where he could watch the sea-birds, and on which his tame geese could paddle. To transport himself around the area Rex built himself a monocoque-style motor cycle that he sat in, instead of on. It had a fibreglass shell and he designed it so that he could go anywhere without goggles and without getting wet. It was fitted with a sidecar, in which his dog would sit as they journeyed around the area.

This motor cycle was just one of Rex's many inventions. Originally from Hillsborough, born in 1915, Rex always enjoyed making things and it is for the making of things that he is famous throughout the world. His list of achievements are too numerous to mention in this book but can be found in Sweet Dreams, The Life and Work of Rex McCandless, by Gordan Small. Amongst many other inventions Rex was responsible for creating "The Benial". The Benial Frame became the basis for all modern day motor cycles. He also masterminded the Mule, a 4-wheel drive cross-country vehicle. In 1959 Rex invented the McCandless Autogyro, a flying machine that required a very short runway. Rex has obviously led a most interesting life and Sweet Dreams is well worth reading.

THE HIB HALL

Back down Memory Lane we venture once again to recall memories of "The Old Hib Hall". The Hibernian Hall, built in 1925, was for many years the centre of entertainment in Killough. The stonemason who built the hall was John Willie Sloan. Anthony Teague remembers how, as a small boy, he and Brian Ward helped labour on the site. "We were only footering about", he recalls, "but we thought we were being helpful."

During the Twelfth Fortnight, when visitors from Belfast invaded the village, several dances

Fisherman's Row, circa 1900 (Hib. Hall on right)

would be held. Music was provided by an accordion band. In the first week of the fortnight the entrance fee was sixpence but in the second week, when money was running short, it was reduced to threepence. The fun was high at these dances and after the dance the young folk would sit out on the Battery Wall and sing the rest of the night away. Dances were also held in a barn behind the coal yard in Carman's Row during holiday time.

Visitors usually came by train from Belfast and the young people of the village would hurry down to the station to meet each train, eager to see who was arriving. Maggie (now Wyatt) and Mary Ellen McIlmale told us that Twelfth Fortnight was the highlight of the year. They rejoiced when the visitors arrived and cried when they went away.

THIS IS A STORY THAT MARY ELLEN TOLD US:

One dark night a man walked home from Downpatrick to Killough. As he walked on he felt something brush against the back of his neck. He turned round to look behind him but saw nothing there. He hurried along and again felt something across the back of his neck. Having heard all the old stories about evil spirits he began to run, by this time thoroughly frightened and convinced that the Devil was after him. When he could run no further he threw himself to his knees and pulled off his hat to bless himself. The strange feeling went away. Relieved, he continued his journey, replacing his hat as he went. Again "the thing" was after him. He pulled his hat off once again, and that was when he discovered that 'the thing' that had tormented him

Receipt for rent, Killough 1799

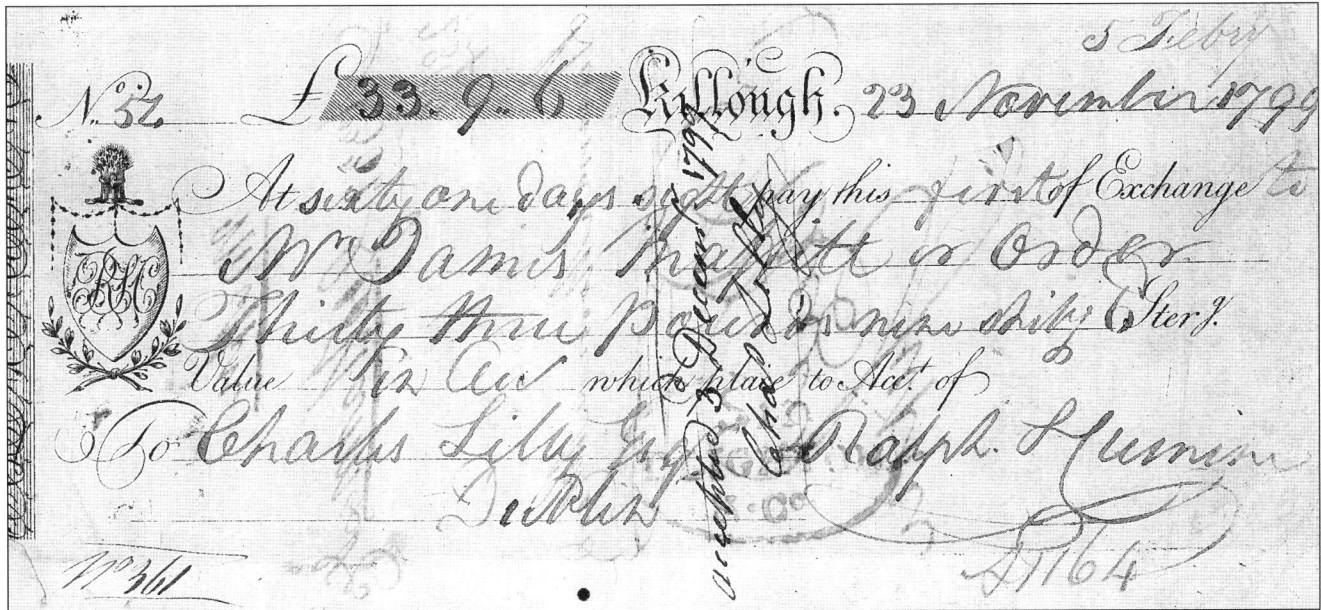

Fisherman's Row, circa 1900

all the way home, was the binding from the brim of his hat, dangling down the back of his neck.

WARTIME TALES

During the Second World War, English and American soldiers were stationed in Killough and German Prisoners of War were up at St John's Point. The soldiers received a warm welcome from many of the local girls who were lonely, their own local boys being away in the armed forces. Many Killough men were in the navy, whilst others were working in England. Dances were held in the Hibernian Hall and St Joseph's Hall. The troops who attended the dances used to love to hear Margaret George (now Clarke) singing Irish ballads. Maggie had a magnificent voice and her renditions of the old Irish songs brought tears to your eyes.

The girls were never short of partners at the dances and several elderly ladies of the village fondly remember being taken home on the bar of a bike, propelled by a "handsome Yank". The Yanks went everywhere on bicycles! The American soldiers were the most popular because they were the ones who could provide chocolates and nylon stockings.

Sadly, many of these American friends were lost when they were posted to Algiers, North Africa. As the soldiers landed they were killed in their hundreds on the beaches there.

Some wartime romances led to marriage. Mary Fitzsimmons was whisked away to Texas by her American husband. She has since returned to the village for a holiday a few years ago.

The soldiers were befriended by the villagers on many occasions. One night a huge American soldier, "a big Mexican", came to Sarah Hanna's door on Fisherman's Row. He came to ask her if she had anything that would cure a sore throat. She heated some salt on the griddle, then taking down a sock that hung on the string over the fireplace, she filled it with the red-hot salt. She slapped the sock round his neck and secured it there with a pin. As the hot salt touched his neck the American let out a mighty yell and attempted to remove the sock. Sarah ordered him to keep it on. The following day he returned to the house and told Sarah that "the Irish magic" had worked. He was completely cured.

During the Black Out there were ARP wardens in the village. One night a warden was stopped by an English soldier and asked:

> *"Where does the woman who makes Shamrock Tea live?"*
> *"What's Shamrock Tea?" asked the warden.*
> *"Tea made with only three leaves." came the reply.*

Killough Post Office, Main Street, circa 1925

Apparently, a woman in the village ran a lucrative business making tea for the soldiers. To increase her profits she made the tea so weak it became known as "Shamrock Tea".

The German Prisoners of War up at the Point may have caused some villagers consternation. One lady, who was resident in Killough during the war, told us "When all the lights were out because of the Black Out, and the mist came in from the shore, I was afraid of the close proximity of the Germans."

Yet another villager tells us, "They were grand lads, hard working and very polite." The POW's were farmed out to local farmers in the area.

THE MARINA?

Patrick Small, a native of Killough, now resident in Royal Windsor, Berkshire, England, told us a lovely story from the time when he was a young man. Patrick is by no means an old man now, this story having taken place in the 1960s.

Benny Gilmore, also a native of Killough, along with his brother Lew, had made a fortune in building, property speculation and horses. He employed the Small brothers, Tom, George and Patrick, also from Killough, at his racing stables in England. Benny loved Killough. He had a vision of how the area could be developed. He believed that the village could become prosperous through tourism. He intended to build a Leisure Park and Marina in Killough. The Leisure Park was to be situated near the four roads crossroads. The Marina was to be in the Bay and the Castle, in Ardglass, was to be turned into a 5-star hotel to accommodate visitors to the area.

At great expense he transported a large consignment of machinery and equipment for draining the land. Along with the machinery came a herd of donkeys, which Patrick had to look after. Faithfully each week Benny sent Patrick his wages and a sack of carrots for the donkeys, by post from England, to arrive every Monday morning at Fisherman's Row.

Sadly, the vision was never to be realised. The machinery lay rusting away, sinking further into the bog land as the years went by. One day, when Benny still nurtured his dream, Patrick received a brown paper packet, delivered by the postman. The packet contained one thousand young fir trees. Benny instructed Patrick to plant the fir trees on the land around the lake at the Strand End, to eventually provide a picturesque setting for the leisure complex. Patrick, knowing very little about landscape gardening, set to and planted all the little trees on the water's edge. Four days later, after torrential rain, the level of the lake rose and all the tiny saplings were washed away never to be seen again, like Benny Gilmore's dream for Killough.

Main Street, circa 1900

KILLOUGH – PORT ST ANNE

The Honourable Michael Ward called the village Port St Anne, and there are some people who prefer that name to Killough. One of these people was Benny Gilmore, who carried out a one-man campaign to have the village officially called Killough-Port St Anne. Here is an extract from a news article that might be of interest to those who favour the name Port St Anne.

A One-Man Crusade

I have just made the acquaintance of a County Down man who is carrying on a most interesting one-man crusade. He is Mr B. Gilmore of Sarajac Cottage, Killough, whose great ambition in life is to see pleasant sounding Killough revert to the even more pleasant sounding Port St Anne, as it was once known. Thus when he writes to me, Mr Gilmore heads his letter Killough-Port St Anne and he would like to see every other Killoughite- I beg your pardon - Killough-Port St Anneite - do the same until the name of Killough-Port St Anne is accepted by the world at large, says Mr Gilmore.

In my opinion, Port St Anne is the more attractive name. It more accurately states the claims of the natural layout and surroundings of the whole port area of Strangford Lough and gives, by its name, a

Denvir's Farm, Crew Road, 1950

A public reply to SIR MAXWELL FYFE, M.P., *at* Westminster & GEO. B. HANNA, M.P., *at* Stormont & others who direct attention *to* CIVIL DEFENCE.

Sirs,

One of the best immediate Civil Defence tryouts is to stop the disgraceful destruction and devastation that continues at the Harbour and Town of peaceful Killough, Port St. Anne, Co. Down., N. Ireland, involving Killough, Port St. Anne's economic survival and property, including a Cemetery.

If this devastation is allowed to go on, then frightening talk about destruction by Atom or Hydrogen bombing leaves us cold and unimpressed; and simply appears another new worm on the old hook.

Will the Civil Defence get a chance to prove itself on this job by orders to restore or stop the damage ?

Or will the Civil Defence prove to be a few good jobs for the Big Boys and forget Killough. Port St. Anne's efforts to live and survive ?

Ben Gilmore, Hon. Sec. The Port St. Anne Society.

Killough. Port St. Anne (a natural Port) in Co. Down, N. Ireland, could amongst many things make an ideal Garden City and suitable for consideration re DISPERSAL OF POPULATION from England etc., particularly the Aged and Blind and thereby make up somewhat for the loss by the Emigration flood of our young people to England etc., through lack of opportunities at home due to causes like the devastation to be seen at Killough, Port St Anne, Co Down eventually wrecking Ulster & Irish Industries, Traders, Shopkeepers and Employees through a lessening home demand for their goods and services :— of course expect the glib speeches from some to deny this truth.

Issued by the Port St. Anne Society.

Printed by J.H.H. Harrow Road, W.2.

Port St Anne Society pamphlet

mental picture in advance of what to expect. Whereas the name Killough from its meaning "Church on the Lough" can only form a very small part of that same area.

The name, Port St Anne, strikes one forcibly as an open advertisement that requires no explanation, and in justice to the Honourable Michael Ward who originated the name in the 17th Century, I think the wisdom of his choice has been proved by time and events. Since the name is no longer used, the trade and industry that once flourished throughout the port has withered away, leaving mementoes of better days and past enterprises all too clearly to be seen in empty and decaying buildings.

Coalboat at Killough Pier, circa 1910

Mr Gilmore proposes that the old name should be revived in such a way that the susceptibilities of the adherents of the name Killough will not be offended - Killough would be retained as part of the postal district within Port St Anne, eg. 'Killough - Port St Anne.'

He even waxes lyrical about it in this attractive poem:

KILLOUGH -PORT ST ANNE

Tis a night of heavenly delight,
The sea subdued, a picture bright;
Silvered by, as only moonlight can,
A shimmering mantle covers Port St Anne.
On nights like this, awaken then,
The wee folk to dance perhaps again;
Alas, not to play, but to plan,
To bring back banished Port St Anne.
In circled conclave they propound.

Castle Street, circa 1900

Our beloved Port, others be confound;
We'll bestir the soul of mortal man
Again to hope in Port St Anne.
So, on a day, it came to pass,
A lady, fair as any lass,
Smiled on everyone in street and lane;
Twas sweet Anne in Port St Anne.
The tale complete is almost told;
Now lovers see their dreams unfold,
When moonlight streams on the fairies' land,
A shimmering mantle covers Port St Anne.

The Motor Car Comes to Killough

The first motor car owner in Killough was possibly Patrick Teague, the father of Anthony, Bobby, Terence and Vincent. The car was a black Model T Ford. It caused quite a stir in the village. Other early car owners were the Parish Priest and Tommy McEvoy. The rest of the village relied upon the bus and train service, either that or they walked. People thought nothing of walking long distances in those days.

When Dr Murphy lived in the house known as Kinvara, he was still doing his rounds on a bicycle. Then he purchased a new car. He was driving home one day when the car was stoned, as it passed along Castle Street, by a young boy who later became a Parish Priest. Father Sean Rogan was reminded of this incident at his ordination. It was said that he didn't much care for these new contraptions coming to Killough.

Mrs Agnes George

Mrs Agnes George is the most senior citizen living in Killough at this time. Originally a citizen of Belfast, she first came to Killough as a young girl. Now in her 91st year, she is the mother of 14 children, grandmother to 48 grandchildren and great-grandmother to 63 great-grandchildren - possibly 64 by the time we go to print. (May 1990)

Henry Patrick Marie Russell-Killough

If you make a trip to Lourdes, and visit the nearby village of Gavarnie, you might be surprised to see a statue bearing the name Henry Patrick Russell-Killough (1834-1903). This statue occupies a prominent place in the village which is a popular outing for visitors to Lourdes. Henry is another famous member of the Russell family of Killough. He was a Papal Count but his fame rests upon his exploration in the Pyrenees. His mother was French and he was born in Toulouse. His vocation for the priesthood was thwarted when he was expelled from Maynooth College for womanising. An extremely eccentric man, he lived in a cave above the snowline on the Pic de Vignamale, one of the highest peaks in the Pyrenees. Wearing full evening dress, he entertained his dinner guests in this unusual abode. He is regarded as the father figure of Pyrennean exploration.

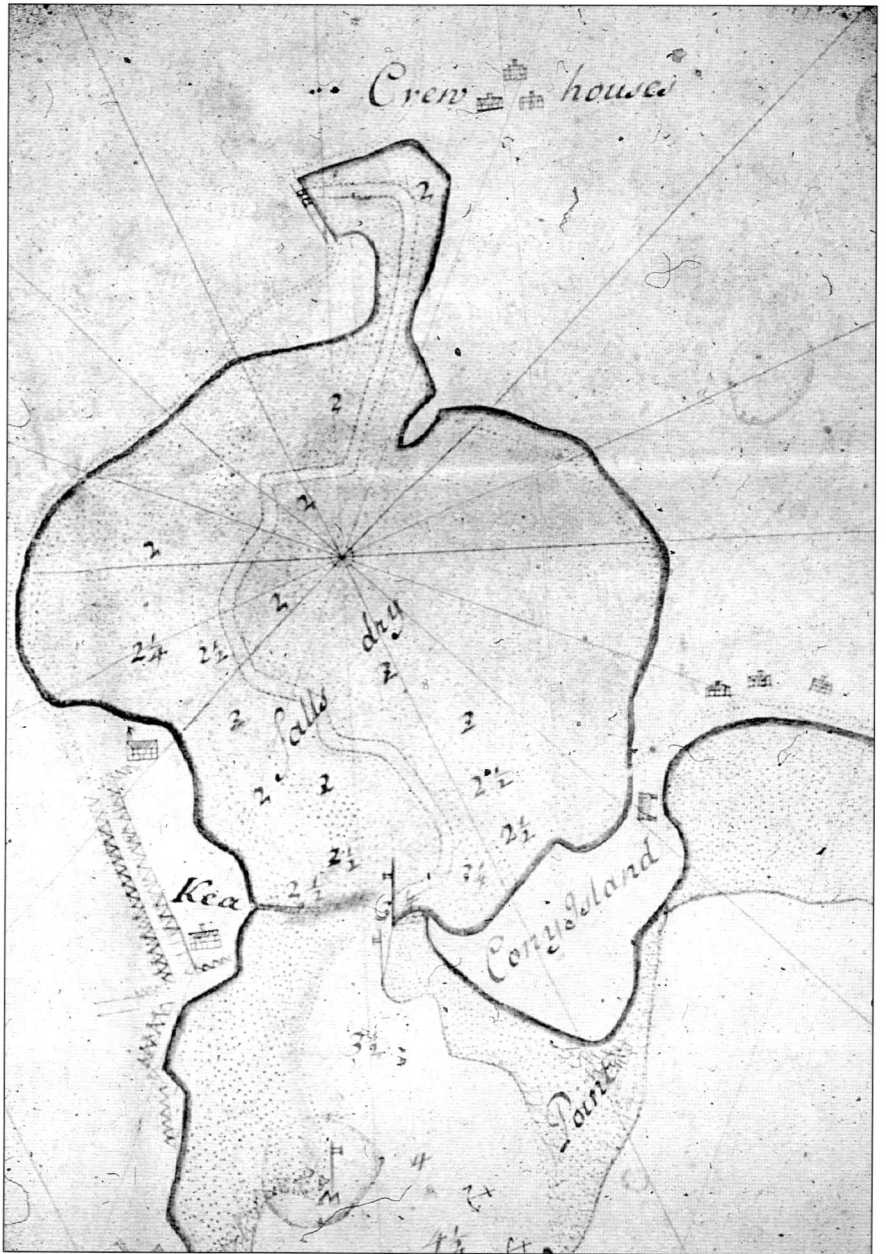

Navigation Maps of Killough 1713.
PRONI D/642/G/1

A Killough Soldier's Tale

The late Cecily Parkinson-Cumine of Killough had in her possession an old, grubby, hand-written notebook that she had discovered in her house. Many of its pages were missing; of those that remained many were torn and in others, the writing had faded to such an extent that it was illegible. What remained, however, was an account of a soldier's adventures in the final months of the Peninsular Wars which ended in 1814, together with a description of his involvement in the Battle of New Orleans which took place in January 1815. The name on the notebook is 'Richard O'Prey, Killough'.

Only two short periods of campaigning are recorded, but at the end of the notebook the soldier writes, 'I am going to give you the number of the general engagements I have been in since the year 1809'. Most were part of the war in Spain between the armies of Napoleon and Wellington. He lists twenty-one battles he was involved in beginning with the battle of Talavera in July 1809, the results of which were indecisive, and ending with the battle of Toulouse on the 10th of April 1814. This was a resounding victory for the English and their Allies over the French under General Soult. O'Prey notes of that battle that 'many were killed and wounded. The loss of the Spaniards was 4,000, the English 2,520, the French 6,000 killed and wounded, 4,000 prisoners'.

It is unclear which regiment Richard O'Prey was a member of, but it seems that he was in one of those groups that had the dangerous task of advancing ahead of the main army and engaging the equivalent group from the French army. The record starts with the English army fighting the French in the Pyrenees and driving them back into France during late 1813. He was fighting in skirmishes nearly every day in the high cold mountains, 'I never suffered so much cold as was there … nothing to shelter us from the cold'. By early October, O'Prey was on French soil and again in almost daily contact with enemy soldiers. On the 11th of October he ran into severe trouble after 'they [the French] got reinforcement and beat us back to a chapel where we kept our ground and fell to work to fortify it working night and day for 6 days. We were forced to dig up the corpses and shelter us with the head stones from the shot of the enemy, drinking water out of the graves and could get no other'. Presumably these corpses were disturbed when they were digging trenches and throwing up banks in order to protect themselves.

Thankfully, Richard and his comrades were soon relieved and set out again on the road to Toulouse where their fortunes greatly changed. 'We then halted in a large village two leagues from Toulouse for eleven days. The inhabitants all fled from it. There we had drumins [?] of wine in every house as good as ever was drank. If you had but seen the soldiers in their glory drinking wine fifty glasses on the table, all full from morning to night. We even washed the horses in wine it was that plenty'. The good life, however, soon came to an end as 'on the 2nd of April at about the hour of 12 midnight we received the orders to advance as far as Toulouse. The ensuring battle left about 7,000 dead or

there the Remained for 6 weeks
making strong works and Batries
this mountain goes by the name
of Larone we found Piquets
every day on it but I never
suffered so much cold as was
there nothing to Shelter us from
the Cold then we Rec'd orders
on the 9 of October to advance
and Drive them from their works
and on the morning of the 10 about
3 Oclock we Made the atack
Drove them from the works inspite
of all their force but we Suffred
a Great Loss we Drove Down
into France to a Place the
Call Arance the Remained for
9 Months and us Close up to them
finding strong out Piquets
every Day their Sentry in

ne Side of the Hege and ours
on the other our Piquots and them
scrimigeen every Day But the
Got a Rain forcement and Beat
us Back to a Chapple there we
Kept our Ground and fell to
work to fortify it working night
and Day for 6 Days we ware
forced to Dig up the Corps and
Shelter us with the head Stones
from the Shot of the Enemy
Drinking the watter out of the
Graves and Could get no other
then we ware Rainforced and
advanced upon them and Drove
them as far a Bayougn there the
Made another Stand for several
Days but we Soon Put them to
the Rout again as far as Sarlers
then we fell in with them again
the 20 of March 1853

Pages from Richard O'Prey's journal

wounded and although the Allies were victorious they suffered more losses than the French. Furthermore, all this slaughter was unnecessary as Napoleon had already abdicated and surrendered but this news had not reached Wellington until an hour after he had taken the town. Richard too was delighted that the long war was over – 'A dragoon came with an address to our General that peace was made between France and England. This was joyful news for the whole army to think their hardships were at an end'. After this Richard and his comrades stayed in Toulouse for another three weeks where he says that the inhabitants treated 'the English soldiers very well'. He is surprised to find that 'a loaf of bread in this place weighed 75 pounds'. From there they marched to the coast and after waiting for a further two and a half months they were taken home to quarters in Plymouth.

If Richard thought his days of danger were over he was mistaken. A new war had begun in America in 1812 and was still continuing in a rather indecisive way. America, noting Great Britain's preoccupations with European wars, decided to try and invade Canada. This proved more difficult than anticipated and when this rather futile war ended in early 1815, all that was proven was that America could not invade and successfully hold Canada, and that the British could not successfully invade and hold America.

Most of the theatre of war was along the American – Canadian border but in late 1814 the Duke of Wellington decided to dispatch his brother-in-law, General Edward Packenham, with an army to the southern states in order to capture New Orleans and remove Louisiana from the United States. Richard O'Prey may not have been too

happy when he received orders for embarkation on the ship Earl of Moria from Plymouth on the 13th of October, on what was to be a disastrous expedition for the British. On the 26th of October they hauled anchor and headed for America. On the 5th December they sailed between the islands of Dominique and Martinique, and from there northward past Guadeloupe and then westwards past Jamaica. Since the soldiers got no chance to land, the only information that Richard could supply was that it 'appear[ed] to be very mountainous near the coast'.

He also found the climate 'extremely warm'. Soon he notes that 'the flying fish is seen in great numbers. They are about the size of a herring'. He also noted that 'the daulphin [dolphin?] is a very beautiful fish especially for its various colours, some weigh thirty and forty pounds weight'. By the 27th of December they were passing Cuba but once again as they cannot land all Richard can report is that 'it seems to be of great extent [but] I cannot give any further account about it'. On the 30th of December they rendezvous with the rest of the fleet that had arrived earlier and sailed north in order to engage in more futile carnage at New Orleans. Peace had already been made between the Americans and British on Christmas Eve but the news had not yet reached the southern armies.

The Battle of New Orleans was to be an unhappy one for the British. The town was well defended by General Andrew Jackson, and much of the fighting took place in the swamps, lakes and rivers around the town. On the 5th of January 1815, Richard found himself encamped on the banks of the river three miles from New Orleans. 'On the 6th we furnished strong working parties to cut a canal for our gun boats to proceed up the river. Both soldiers, sailors and marines were employed on this occasion which was very laborious'.

There then ensured an artillery duel between the two sides. Because of the muddiness of the ground, Richard noted that it 'obliged us to build our batteries of 'shugar' instead of sand' – presumably this was sugar cane chopped down in the vicinity! The British artillery made little headway. New Orleans was well defended by a lake on its western side, and as Richard says, the 'enemy having stationed in this lake a frigate and several gun boats for the protection of the town', their artillery was thus much more flexible than that of the British.

On the 6th of January the main engagement between the two armies begun. Luckily for Richard, he seems to have remained in the relative safety of his sugar cane battery. He reports the battle as follows; 'on the evening of the same day the enemy sallied out and rush[ed] into the camp with rapidity whilst the soldiers were employed in refreshing themselves. Immediately the 95th and the 93rd got under arms and with little loss on their side soon made the enemy retire in great confusion leaving many dead on the field. I am sorry today to regret the loss of a few brave officers and soldiers of the above corps on this occasion'.

His description continues, 'nothing else happened during that night. Next morning the enemy kept a continual fire from the batteries and from a frigate and gun boats … which annoyed our working parties very much, all necessary preparations being made for a general attack'. Richard spent the night of the 7th as part of these preparations for a final attack on the town and records that he 'finished a battery of nine guns'. It was a busy night as all the troops of the various regiments had to take up positions for the attack on the following day – 'the army was to be drawn in close order near as possible to the enemy … to arrive at their appointed stations about 11 o'clock on the night of the 7th so as to commence the engagement a little before daybreak on the morning of the 8th. A rocket was to be thrown up at that hour as a signal to engage in all quarters'.

At first the battle seemed to go well for the British. Richard O'Prey records 'the 85th regiment, with sailors and marines, crossed the river before day break in armed boats and landed without being perceived by the enemy and took possession of two forts without any considerable loss'. The other attacks, however, were much less successful. Attempts to take two of the town bastions by 'a storming party of 300 men' led, as Richard records, to 'great loss for want of sufficient support'. The main defences of the town were attacked by five regiments, one of which the 44th carried 'scaling ladders and bridges', but again this proved 'unsuccessful on account of the depth and breadth of a ditch that was thrown up in front of the enemy's position'.

In fact at this stage the British were in considerable difficulty and, as often is the case, a scapegoat had to be found to account for their misfortunes. O'Prey states that Commander of the Forces, General Packenham, 'observing the misconduct of the 44th regiment … rode up immediately, but before he could reach the spot I am sorry to say that he received his death wound and was immediately taken to the rear'. Before he died, the General, realising that all was lost ordered the army to retreat. Richard played a part in this retreat as he records that, in order to render abandoned artillery useless to the enemy, he 'spiked a nine gun battery and retreated in regimental form to the former encampment'. There the defeated British army had to remain 'under a constant fire of their heavy cannon for ten days'. The misery ended when news came from the north that a treaty had been signed between the two sides on Christmas Eve. It can hardly have raised the spirits of O'Prey and his comrades that the whole bloody defeat at New Orleans had been unnecessary. The journal states 'you must consider our uncomfortable situation here … besides the coldness of the weather added more to our miseries'. There was, however, some comfort as he records 'every day we were poured out [a] half pint of spirits per man which was a great service to the health of the troops'.

On the 19th of January, O'Prey and his comrades moved down river and came to a small island where they encamped. 'The length of this island was three miles … and is a complete wilderness. At the open end of it there are a few shabby huts, the residence of a few Spaniards who were fishermen. Their habitations were occupied by the staff of the army'. He continues 'the climate is extremely warm besides. All tormented with a kind of fly called meskittys [mosquitoes]. We destroyed a number of alligators here. They are of ordatious size. Their head is like a calf only flatter. The under jaw never moves. The tail is like a fish and his fore paws are like a Christian. Hardly anything can pierce their skin'. He had plenty of time to observe the wildlife, 'too tedious to mention we remained there to the 4th of April'.

Finally, they began to head for home but the prevailing winds necessitated a rather circuitous route. By the 8th of April they were within sight of Havana in Cuba but they then had to head northwards. On the 3rd of May they hit a dreadful storm and 'many of our ship's sails were torn in pieces. We lost the fleet on the same night'. Soon Richard's ship was to encounter more trouble. On the 27th of May 'it being very tempestuous we were near loosing our foremast' somewhere off the Banks of Newfoundland, and the following day 'to our great astonishment we perceived several ordatious? mountains of ice floating on the sea'. For a while they were lost but they manage to arrive back in Plymouth by the 5th of June nearly eight months after they had left for their ill-fated campaign in America. We know nothing of what happened O'Prey after this but presumably he returned to live out his life in Killough. O'Preys continue to live in the village to this day and perhaps Richard was an ancestor of Danny O'Prey who was the cox of the Killough Lifeboat at the beginning of the (present) last century.

A KILLOUGH SAILOR'S TALE

Over three hundred letters of James C. Parkinson have survived and they provide a unique and detailed account of a sailor and emigrant's life in the latter half of the nineteenth century.

James C. Parkinson was born in Killough in 1832. His father was a Church of Ireland minister from Armagh and his mother was of an old Killough family. The family was moderately wealthy their income being derived from the rents of the townland of Grangecam, near Downpatrick, which his mother had inherited. James was the eldest and there were grand plans to for him to go to Trinity College in Dublin to study medicine. He went to primary school locally but after a few years it was decided to pack him off to boarding school in Dungannon.

Boarding school, however, did not suit James who was a bit of a loner. Within a few weeks of his arrival he was getting into fights with the other pupils. To add to his troubles he was also the victim of petty theft from his schoolmates. He was also a poor student and was especially weak in Greek and Latin which was necessary for the study of medicine. Home too was not much fun as his parents seemed to have been extremely strict and he preferred to visit his uncle Edward in Armagh rather than go back to Killough during term breaks.

His second year at college proved to be as academically unsuccessful as his first and within a few weeks his father decided to move him from Dungannon and send him instead to a school in Armagh. The headmaster at Dungannon found it necessary to defend his school from accusations of poor standards of teaching in his correspondence

James C. Parkinson

with James' father arguing that his son's poor progress was due to his "idleness and inattention".

> "I should be the first to blame the assistant who taught his class, were it not that four boys, viz. Stewart, Blacker, Stokes and Tatton, out of a class of six, improved remarkably under his care and answered every repetition exceedingly well in their Greek grammar. Richards, a very idle boy, made some progress, and James, the sixth made none. I cannot therefore blame the assistant".

Armagh proved to be of little benefit as far as his studies were concerned and within a year the headmaster, a Mr Lister, is writing to his father stating that, "I am exceedingly displeased with James", stating that he was acting and "scheming most disgracefully", and that he was "impossibly lazy". Angry letters were exchanged between father and son. Additionally, James' mother wanted to bring him home as the expense of keeping him in boarding school begun to seem a little pointless especially as the father was now working as a minister in County Louth which necessitated the keeping of two houses.

In order to save money the family decided that they could no longer afford the luxury of a horse but when they decided to sell a pleasure boat they owned we get the first inkling of James' interest in the sea. He wrote to his sister Frances noting that:

"I received your note a day or to ago and was very sorry that the large boat was sold. I felt very sorry indeed! I hope that dada will not part with the small one. Many a pleasant day I spent in her and I seemed to feel that I had lost a friend".

Letters sent by his Killough school friend Joe Surch of nautical goings-on at home must have also made him restless. In one such letter in December 1849 Joe describes an unusual shipwreck off Killough.

"We were all surprised last night by the appearance of a vessel on fire off Killough. The night was so dark we could see but little. Four of the Scordon boats went off to her and about an hour after the coast guards (after bringing their boat on a car from the quay to Scordon) but she returned in two hours saying the vessel was too far off and drifting faster than they could pull. They went five or six miles and they supposed the fire to be fifteen. This is all we could learn at 11 o'clock. On this morning we learned that Capt. Gelpie Don Juan of Dundalk had the sailors on board six in number (but I should say that she came in to Killough after we went to bed). One of the sailors is a black. She left

Christina Parkinson and child, circa 1865

Liverpool and was put into Belfast with bad weather and left that port for the Mediterranean with a general cargo. The vessel belongs to the Capt. and worth £1600 and only partly insured. No one can tell how the fire begun. It became visible at 6 o'clock and she sank at 12 o'clock. This is all I can learn respecting the thing".

Letters from parents and his grandmother, along with the admonitions of his headmaster, has accomplished little in improving his studies and in late 1850 the family solicitor, Mr Gracey, got involved in trying to make James improve his studies. He wrote a patronising letter beginning "I happened incidentally to learn you were not making any considerable progress in the studies so indispensable to your creditable entrance into Trinity College" and ending up with "You are still inexperienced, but you have the example of your amiable and excellent father, which I trust you will probably appreciate, and in following his footsteps and taking him as your guide, you will qualify yourself throughout life to discharge all your important duties, religious, moral, and social. That this may be the case is the sincere wish and hope of, Your friend, J. Gracey".

All this was of no avail and in the middle of 1851 James had abandoned school and was enquiring about careers in the bank and in the police, but soon his mind was set on going to sea. This horrified his pompous and class snobbish father who feared that mixing with lowly sailors would corrupt and mislead his son. He tried to get James enlisted as a midshipman to a Liverpool ship called the "Royal Stewart" in order to avoid this dreadful situation. He was indeed assured by the ship's representative that he would not have to mix with the ordinary sailors.

James Parkinson and family in Tasmania, circa 1810

"It is understood that the Midshipmen have intercourse with and associate with the Captain and passengers that they are kept entirely from the men. As to your fancying they mess with a lower class, I think that my letter stated they would live and mess with the 3rd officer who was previous to this promotion a Midshipmen. In the Indiaman the 1st and 2nd officers mess with the Captain and the Midshipmen mess with the third officers. They have no menial duty to perform. Their employment will be upon ships duty only by which they shall learn their profession. The "Royal Stuart" the ship we offered is a new vessel. You could not have a finer ship in one in which your son could learn his profession better". (8/9/51).

James finally headed for Liverpool in early October on a steamer from Belfast. He wrote to his mother informing her that most of the passengers were sea-sick but that he, of course, was not. He did not, however, join the "Royal Stewart" but instead fell in with a captain from Downpatrick called Scott who took him on as an apprentice. His father's attempts to stop him associating with lowly sailors had clearly failed as James was now joining the seagoing career at the bottom rung of the ladder. James announced to his mother that he was sending his good suit home from Liverpool as it would be spoiled at sea, and thus begun his seagoing life. His first voyage in the Dalriada, as Captains Scott's ship was called, was with a cargo of coal to India.

We next hear of James in Bombay in early March 1852 where he reports that ship had hit the "fag end of a hurricane" near Mauritius which tore away nine of their sails. "The vessel rolled tremendously. One would think that she would never rise again and when we went below the house on deck where the boys live such a mess there was, the harness casks had broken adrift and all the beef and pork was rolling from side to side amongst about a cart load of paint pots and paints that had been stowed". One of the blankets from his hammock ended up in the paint. He then talks of

Rates bill, Killough, 1820

calling at Ceylon for bananas, coconuts and pineapples. India, not surprisingly, is hot and he wrote home vivid descriptions of the city and its inhabitants. He summarised his impressions by writing "I was ashore and saw a great number of queer people and curious things".

James C. Parkinson's seaman's docket

The ship's dog, however, did not take well to Bombay. "The Capt. brought a large Newfoundland Dog with him and he did very well until we came into Harbour, where in a few days he went mad, but fortunately did no harm altho he was racing fore and aft the decks as if a dozen tin pots were after him but his career was ended by a leaden bullet from the mates fowling piece".

It was to be a month before Captain Scott could find a buyer for his cargo of coal and during that time James was allowed on shore only twice. The unloading of the cargo was a dismal task and took three weeks to complete – "I hope never to be shipmates with such a one again, as everything is covered with coal dust, which being so dry penetrates and it is only on Sunday that you would know to what class of beings we belong".

Having unloaded the ship was unable to obtain goods to trade and they were stranded in Bombay for three or four months. Captain Scott dismissed his European crew keeping only four, James included. The fact that James' parents knew the captain probably saved him from a similar fate. In September the Dalriada set sail for Wampoa in China with a cargo of cotton. His letters show that the novelty of the sailors life was now wearing thin and he showed little understanding of the culture and people of China.

> "No European is allowed to go into the town of Wampoa, but there are other villages close around it where you can if you are civil. But should you kick up any row you may look out for yourself, as the Chinese are the most savage bloodthirsty rascals ever were created and they think as little of taking a life as of killing a rat. But 'tis no wonder as the devil is their God."

From China the boat headed to Hong Kong and Singapore and on to Indonesia where it took on a cargo of sugar which was to be brought to Amsterdam. Christmas day found him anchored in the port of Batavia and longing for home, "I am long tired of this ship and indeed a sailor's life". He had now been over a year at sea, the previous Christmas day having being spent off the Cape of Good Hope, and it was not until June that they arrived in Amsterdam. From there he writes that Captain Scott has given him enough money for a new suit and asks his sisters to make up some new shirts for him for his next voyage.

His arrival home in Killough in September must have been spoiled by the fact that Captain Scott had written beforehand to James' mother informing her of his behaviour in Amsterdam.

"The subject on which I have now to address you is to me a very painful one and I am sure to you will be more so, up to our arrival in Amsterdam James conducted himself remarkably well, but no sooner had we got to Newdeep that he appeared to loose all regard for himself scarcely a day passing that he was not drunk, going on shore and stopping away all night and on one occasion he absented himself for three days and nights from the ship and that in company of the lowest blackguards he

The Parkinson family home, Castle Street

could meet. I repeatedly cautioned him on the course he was pursuing and even threatened to write to his Grandmother but all to no use. I have advanced him about £10 over and above also his wages which amount to about £9 no inconsiderable sum for a young man in his situation at sea (as much as I had for the whole time of my apprenticeship) but notwithstanding all that he is very bare of clothes. I am afraid to let him have any more for fear he puts it to an improper use. At Newdeep I gave him £5 to buy clothes but a day or two before we left the bill came in to me to pay as he had spent all he had got in the latter end of the week. I will be able to let him leave, but if there is not a great refreshing in his conduct I could not think of taking him out again for fear of the influence it might have over the conduct of some young lads I was going to take out next voyage".

Unsurprisingly he stayed at home only a week and was soon heading back to Birkenhead near Liverpool to rejoin the Dalriada from where he writes to his father that "I am exceedingly grieved by the sorrow I have caused and indeed I am not worthy to have you as my parents, but I hope that brighter days will come". The ship this time sailed westward and by the end of February 1854 he had arrived in San Francisco. There he jumped ship claiming in a letter home that the Captain had mistreated him on the voyage. He added that he was joining an American ship for a voyage to the Philippines.

We do not now what James did after this but the next we hear from him is in September 1856 when we find that he is digging for gold in New South Wales in Australia. There he remained for three years continually writing home stating that he was soon about to strike it rich. A one stage he met someone that he knew from Armagh during this school days who got James employment at the shop where he worked but the lure of the goldfields soon had James back digging from his fortune. By the autumn of 1857 he had had enough and fled Australia and headed from home. From the ship Norfolk he wrote to his mother.

> "I met with an accident at the claim and was not able to work … The claim has turned out nothing so I thought the best thing I could do was to come home as I am sick of working for nothing and think that I have tried my luck pretty well. I would not spend five years like the preceding ones again for all the wealth of Victoria. Perhaps I shall be able to find something to do at home for I can tell you that I have had my fill of rambling. I have not got money enough to buy clothes and get home any way respectable so could you manage to send me a few pounds".

James stayed in Killough and considered the idea of starting a career in farming. He contemplates taking on some of the family Grangecam lands and of buying more lands. James knew nothing of farming but his Uncle Edward in Armagh, after much discussion with some farming friends, advised James that it was too much of a risk. He concluded that if the venture did not go well James would certainly loose on his investment. Late in the year he appears to had given up on trying to make living at home. He also seems to have been causing trouble due to his fondness of the bottle and he had to apologise to his mother, his father being dead a few years, for his "outrageous conduct" but adding that "I have felt the sinfulness and selfishness of my conduct and I am determined by God's help to lead a new life". For a month he tried some short distance coasting work in the Irish Sea but by December he was back in Liverpool and signed up on a ship, the Marbatan, bound for New Zealand and Australia where he intended to settle. While in Liverpool he took lodgings in a Mr Montgomerys who seemed to be friend of the family. He wrote to James mother stating of James that "there is not the slightest appearance of drink having passed his lips". His wayward ways seemed to be over and his letters show him becoming very religious in his outlook.

The Marbatan, however, not head to Australia but instead traded for most of 1861 it traded between Calcutta, Mauritius and Burma. He is not enjoying this, he is praying a lot, avoiding drink and once again thinking of returning to Killough to try again to start a new life. He also suffered from an "abscess in the stern" which must have added to his general despondency. At the end of the year the Captain of the Marbatan decided to head for England instead of heading to Australia. He landed in Falmouth in late June and took a train to Liverpool to where his mother and one of his sisters had come to meet him. Within a month, however, he was back in Liverpool joining a new ship, the Almora, although it is not clear if this was as a crew member or as a paying passenger. By early November, however, he had finally made it to Melbourne, Australia.

He thinks about the gold digging again but decides against it and instead headed to Hobart in Tasmania where he joined a brig, the Prairie, that traded between there and New Zealand. This was to be only a short term plan as he intended to settle down as soon as possible "The Captain is the best man ever I sailed with and a teetotaller and no one could desire better than we get to eat. Beautiful white bread, fresh meat, potatoes, plum duff etc. I mean to stop in her until I have some money and I think this place or the neighbourhood of it will suit very well to settle ashore". James spent most of the next two years trading between New Zealand and Tasmania with occasionally journeys to Australia. He also some periods ashore where he stayed in lodgings and he begun to attend the local Methodist church.

Tasmania was a great fruit growing area and on some of his visits to Rockhampton, Queensland, James decided to do some private fruit trading in order to supplement his sailors income. On one voyage in July 1863 he sold fruit at Rockhampton, Queensland, for three time what he had paid for it in Tasmania. In another instance he sold fruit and fish he bought for £6 for £20 at Newcastle in New South Wales.

James very much liked being shore and from early 1863 his thoughts turned to finding a wife writing to his mother that "I hope to fall in with some respectable person soon as I am sick of this unsettled kind of life". The constant sailing, however, was not conducive to this hope being realised. In late November of that year, however, an ailment that had been troubling him from some time got worse "I went to the highest medical practitioner here Dr Crowther and he told me that the disease was Fistula and I had better get it cut out which was done and I am able to walk about again thank God but I shall not be able to go to work again for some time". This gave the opportunity to the now reformed and deeply religious James to spend more time socialising with people on shore in Hobart. A month later he is reporting to his mother:

"I have kept myself very circumspect since I have been here and the few who I am acquainted with are of the better class. I have become acquainted with a young person here who I think would make as far as I can judge a very good wife, as she has one essential thing in her possession the fear and love of God. The only objection that I can see is that her parents are poor but respectable and religious and in a new country like this I do not think it matters so much whether we are well connected so long as we belong to Jesus Christ's own nobility… You can give me your thoughts on the subject. I am not in a hurry to put a halter on this involvement yet".

The object of James' amorous interest was a certain Rebecca Speakman but he soon had to leave again for the sea. In early January 1864 he joined a brig called the Dart and was once again sailing between Tasmania and New Zealand. He sent a photograph of Rebecca to his mother in Killough adding that "she has rather disfigured her countenance to keep in the laughing but I do not intend anything serious until I am in a better position than at present, as three months ashore ran away with some cash". The journey to New Zealand usually only took a week so James would have been able to visit his fiancée at fairly regular intervals. There was still, however,

no decent employment on shore that would allow him abandon sailing and he told his mother that he should not get "spliced" until he had could give up sailing and have something more permanent on shore. Despairing of attaining this in Hobart he tried some shore work in June in Auckland, New Zealand. He found the place disagreeable, "I do not like this place at all so much mud in the streets one is up to the ankles and sometimes to the knees" and "Board is £1-5-0 a week here and that of the coarsest description". He speculated that he would also try shore work in Australia but instead decided to make a long voyage that would give him an opportunity to raise some decent cash to use as capital for settling ashore. He joined a barque called the Dispatch and by early December he was in Ningpo, in China from where he announces that "I hope I will be settled before this time next year".

A month later he was in Saigon, Vietnam "60 miles up a river and very hot" and "sorry that I came so far from Australia but I did not think the voyage would be so long". By April he was in Hong Kong, and from there the Dispatch headed for Manilla, and then by July on to Shanghai with a cargo of sugar they had brought from the Philippines. All he wanted to do at this stage was to go to Australia, get married and settled down. A serious setback occurred, however, as the Dispatch sailed down the Yangtze river bound for Fou-Chou-Fou. The Captain had been trading in this area for some time and decided he would not use a pilot. The boat struck the shore and while all the crew were saved the ship was a total loss.

James managed to get another ship, the Anita, which was to sail to Japan and then to New York but unfortunately he developed a swelling in his thumb, had to go to hospital in Shanghai, a town which he describes as "the most disagreeable place ever I have been in". The Anita sailed without him, he could not get any work and was having to spend thirty five shillings a week for lodgings. He was stranded in Shanghai for at least two months but somehow he managed to get to Melbourne, Australia, by early December. In a state of total despondency, however, instead of heading for Hobartown and his sweetheart he instead decided to head home to his mother and family in Killough.

1st December 1865

Dearest Mamma

You will be surprised to hear that I am coming home. I find it impossible to stay any longer from home. I have had a great deal of roughing it in this country. People at home have no notion of it whatever. In fact this country is as bad in respect to wages as home. I am coming home in the Roxborough Castle bound for London. I am starting tomorrow. I need not tell you what I have come through. I will have a good yarn for a winter night round the fire. I am so sick and tired of this country without a friend to speak to and when I did get work it was of the very hardest kind at 6s a week in a burning sun from any daylight to dark. I expect to arrive in London about the end of February. I am working my way home as cook mate. You need not write any letters for I should not get them. Oh I know what it is to have a home now so keep up your spirits.

Dear Mamma, I remain your affect son,

J.C. Parkinson.

There seemed to have been few attractions at home and by May 1866 James has back in Horbarttown after being eighteen months away. "I am back in the old place once more and it appears like a second home, for of any place I have been there is not any I like as well as this always barin the 'old sod'". Alas, however, his sweetheart was not waiting. James' claimed to his mother that he had ended their relationship but the reasons given seem rather unconvincing. "The lady that has been my intended when I was away in China was told by a relation of hers from Melbourne when she saw my likeness that I was a married man, and had a wife and two children and that my name was Mulligan. So as she was so weak as to give credit to such a falsehood I have not spoken to her since and don't intend". It seems more likely that Rebecca tired of waiting for him to come back from China and had gone off with someone else.

James however was not wasting time for he also told his mother "I have been recommended to a person who seems suitable to make me a good wife" and that he had "been introduced to a Miss Christina Coates who as far as I can judge is the right sort to make a good wife. She is of English parents born, I believe in India, and a member of the Church of England". He was still not able to get a job on shore but by the end of July he had met up again with his teetotal friend Captain Hopkins who appointed him as second mate to his ship called the Picard and soon he was trading with nearby ports.

Having lost one potential wife by resolving to settle down on shore before marrying he was determined not to make the same mistake and he and Christina were married before the end of the year. The wedding was a small affair, "We had not many at the wedding only the immediate friends and relations, Mr and Mrs Sculthorpe officiated and we had our déjeuner at Christina's mothers and a carriage conveyed the party to and from the church". They rented a red-brick cottage with three rooms, a kitchen and an outside well. While still at sea the journeys were short and James' clearly enjoyed the domestic life he had so long wanted, "I must say that Chris does everything to make me comfortable and happy and am confident that I could not have made a better choice". He had some money tied up in Killough and he wrote to his mother, "I hope you will approve of me sending for the rest of the money as I am thinking of going into a little business and it is always best to begin in ones own capital".

Alexander Nimmo's map of Killough and Ardglass coast, 1821

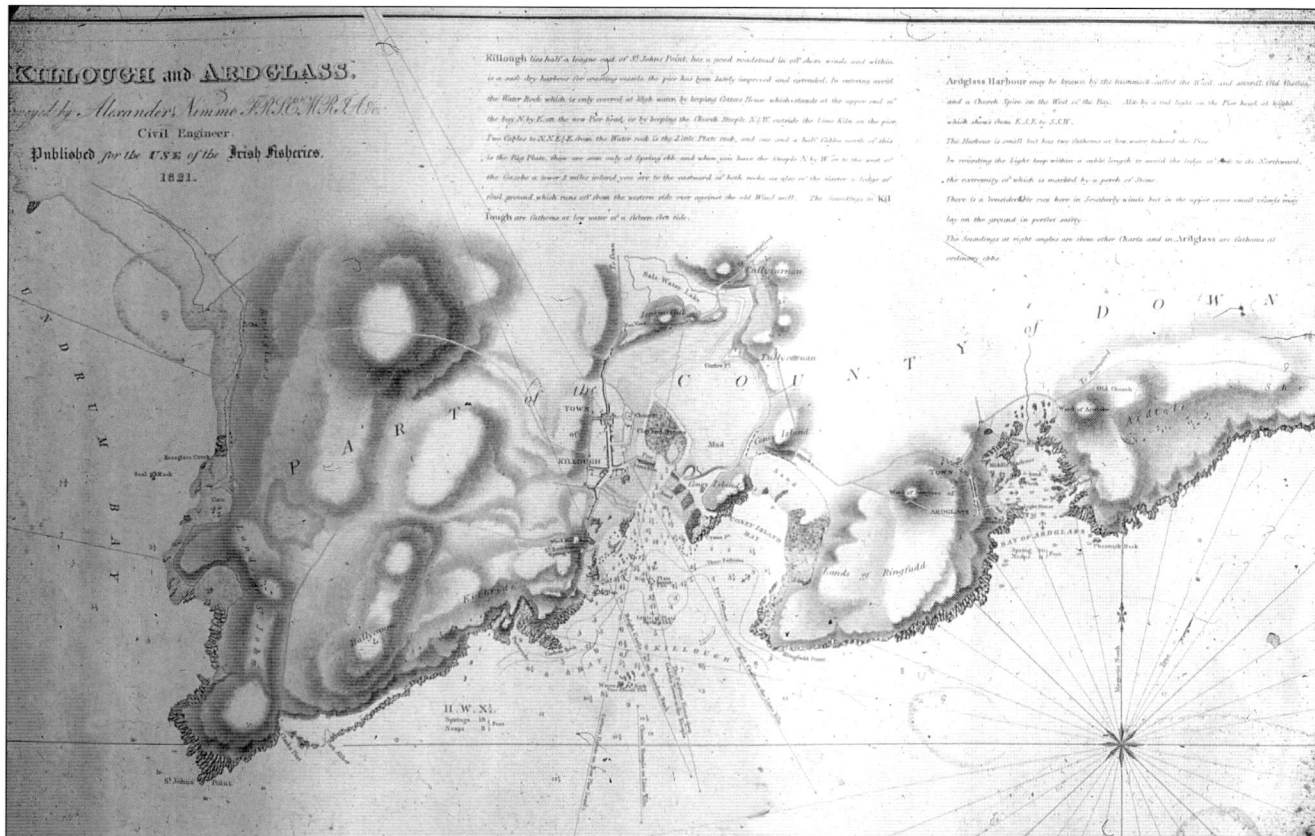

Early in 1867 James was forced ashore because his friend Captain Hopkins began to suffer from a bad liver and had to retire from the sea. By July James had set up his own business taking over a vegetable store from someone who had left Hobartown. Christina was pregnant and it looked as if James' sailing days were over, "I thank God that I am able to leave that nasty sea" James wrote to his mother in July. As the pregnancy progresses Christina becomes more apprehensive writing to Killough that "so many of my young friend have been called [to God] at the trying hour and others have lost their dear babys. May the Lord grant that it will not be my case for dear James sake for he is quite proud to think that he is going to be a papa". In July they had though that the baby would arrive in November but it not until the end of January 1868 that the child, a daughter, was born, after fifteen hours of labour on Christina's part. "She is a splendid child and I hope to be able to do my duty to her" wrote James proudly to his mother. They named her Annie after James' mother. Alas, business at the shop was extremely slow and the profits could not support the family, "The shop we had was in the principal street and the rent and expenses were too high for the business that we did but I hope that we will be able to get over it. We did not loose anything worthwhile by bad debts". By July he was back on a ship, the steamer City of Hobart S.S, and was sailing between Hobart and Sydney.

Throughout 1868 and 1869 James fell into a pattern of working on shore, when employment was available, and returning to sea when it was not. The work was probably of a menial type as he does not give any details of it in the letters home. The family also moves accommodation a few times and by December 1869 they were in a cottage on the edge of town which had a garden attached. He had also steady employment on shore at this time and he wrote home, "I hope that I will not have to go to sea again". They kept some fowl in the garden and in the hope of providing vegetables for the family James wrote to his mother for seed from Killough, "please send me a few seeds of 'curly cabbage' in your letter".

Besides getting seed from Killough James had many strong, and practical, connections with home. He received a constant stream of Downpatrick and Belfast newspapers to read. His brother Samuel had become a doctor and James had pills and prescriptions sent to Tasmania. In early 1870 he joined a local Orange Lodge and had his regalia and sent to him from Killough, "Remember the O scarf is to be orange and purple as I have taken that degree" he wrote in June of that year. By September of that year a son had arrived who was unsurprisingly Christened William. September was also their Spring and James was also able to announce that the "cabbage seed all came up and plants look well".

James never had to return to the sea after this although in June 1871 he found himself in great difficulties. He wrote home "I have now been nearly a month without employment and rent and expenses going on. I do not see any prospect but to take to my old profession which is not very agreeable and is only a bare livelihood and as for saving money here it is out of the question". Things had not improved much by August. "You may form some idea of the state of matters when I tell you that I have not had a full weeks work in three months and I am not as bad in that respect as many others. It is a great trial to be able and willing to work and to be unable to get employment". His membership of the Orange Order, however, had practical advantages in these difficult times, "Thanks to the kindness of some of the 'Brethren' we have not wanted". Mother in Killough too helped by sending him out money. The following month he managed to get work again but employment remained very irregular for most of the following twelve months.

James' career again took a distinctly maritime turn in August 1873 when he was appointed to a boat crew of the Marine Department. At last, a steady job had materialised and James was clearly delighted, especially that another son, George, had recently arrived. The Orange Order connections had yet again had proved advantageous,

> "Wages 28/- per week, house, firing and £6 a year allowed for clothes, which situation I have been appointed to about a fortnight ago through the influence of a brother Orangeman named James Weir of Belfast with a Mr Babington, the harbour master formerly of Londonderry and acquainted with the old Capt. Cotter. It is a great relief to us as I have been a good deal put about lately and it will take us some time to get straight again. I hope that I feel grateful to Him who superintends the affairs of us poor mortals for his goodness to us as I have been a good deal put about lately and it will take us some time to get straight again. I hope that I feel grateful to Him who superintends the affairs of us poor mortals for his goodness to us as I had no prospect of employment for some time. The work is very light principally boarding every ship coming in. In fact I could not have anything to suit me better.

A year later James was promoted again and became a lighthouse man on the Iron Pot light where he remained until his death in 1887 at the age of 54. In the meantime he had several more children and he continued to write to his mother and family in Killough informing of the progress of his life. He took up jam making as a hobby and used to ship pots of it half way around the world to his Killough home. In return they made jam from the fruits of their garden in Castle Street, Killough and sent it to him. The letters that he wrote home constitute the biggest collection from a single person between Australia and Ireland during the nineteenth century and can be read on the internet at the following address. http://www.qub.ac.uk/arcpal/local/killough/index.html

THE EARLY PIER IN KILLOUGH

The pier that stands today in Killough was designed by the Scottish engineer Alexander Nimmo for Lord Bangor in about 1820. The earliest map of Killough, dating to 1716, shows a small straight pier on the site of the present structure. This was obviously too small for Michael Ward's ambitions for the village as he intended developing Killough as an important port for maritime trade. In the spring of 1736 his agent, Frances Lascelles, began to supervise the rebuilding of the pier and details of the work can be found in the correspondence between the two. From the outset there were continual problems both with the availability of stone and with the foundations to the pier. Lascelles notes at one stage that "we sunk all the foundation stones a little in the clay which was troublesome with sand washing [in with] every tide". In some cases the clay was too soft and the agent complained that he could not find a foundation. These deep foundations were also problematical because of the difficulties of getting mortar to set underwater and he complained that "the mortar under the water must be very rich but we are as sparing of the lime as possible".

A lime kiln had been built near the pier to produce lime mortar for the building work[1]. Sometimes there was an abundance of lime and at one stage, Frances Lascelles reported that after burning the lime kiln for eight days the storage house was filled with slaked lime and coal. At other time the scarcity of lime put a halt to the building work. The nearest source of lime was Carlingford but at times it was not readily available from that source. On one occasion the shortage of limestone

Grainstore on the beach, circa 1950

71

for mortar was so acute in Killough that Frances Lascelles sent someone to Gun's Island at Ballyhornan in order to try and find some limestone outcrops but the geology of the area made it extremely unlikely that this search was successful.

Working on the pier was difficult and poorly paid work. During the summer of 1736 there were twenty eight labourers employed on the quay working seven hours in the morning and three in the afternoon, the exact time of the shifts depending on the state of the tides. When the tide curtailed work the labourers were employed in drawing stone to the pier. Pay was 4d a day with food included and 6d if you supplied your own.

Although the daily overseeing of the work was generally undertaken by Frances Lascelles, Michael Ward was constantly kept in touch with developments and approached for advice when needed. In May 1736, Lascelles can be found writing to Ward looking for advice on the positioning of the slipway and on the layout of the steps down the side of the pier. To finish the work 'stoops' were needed to be embedded along the pier edge so that ships' ropes could be attached to them. Lascelles was of the opinion that these had to be of oak but lets Ward know that no oak is available locally and suggests that he might find some in Dublin to ship to Killough.

Instructions for sailing into Killough, 1713. PRONI D/642/G/1

Killough sloop running into the harbour in a storm 1735, by Leslie Jones (1999)

Stone for the work was obtained from a number of local quarries and seems to have been acquired in a rather ad hoc fashion. In May 1736, we learn form Lascelles that he has "got a parcel of very fine paving stones from Mr Harroll's land" but the location of this is not known. Some of the largest stones were brought from the Castle Park about one mile south of Killough and some were so big that they necessitated six horses to drag them from the Park to the quay. At other times, stone was quarried from the opposite shore of the bay on Coney Island and the remains of the quarry can be clearly seen today behind the house known as 'The Moorings'.

In addition to the masonry stone, large quantities of loose infill were needed for the pier. This seems to have been transported in carts known as 'tumblers' and also in tubs of some types. The latter were not a success and needed constant mending of the 'hooping'. These were becoming too costly to maintain and it was suggested that 'creels' made of 'scallops', presumably sally rods, would be much cheaper for the purpose. A letter was duly sent to Michael Ward asking if he would like to change to these and if his authority was given, the labourers would be set to make them.

The finished pier was not without its problems. In 1739, a spring and quicksand began to undermine the quay wall and a bulge appeared in face that raised the possibility that some of the edifice would have to be dismantled and rebuilt. This, however, was a relatively minor consideration when compared to the basic flaw in the whole concept of building a pier at Killough, i.e., that when the tide was out the whole bay virtually emptied and it could not be used for shipping.

This inconvenience greatly concerned the ship owners of the village. In 1738, these numbered ten, including Frances Lascelles, and between them they owned fifteen ships ranging between fourteen and thirty-seven tons in weight. The ships for the most part had personal names such the 'Nancy', 'Happy Nancy', 'William', 'Michael', 'William and Mary', 'John and Mary', the exceptions to this rule being the 'Oak', 'Industry' and 'Three Brothers'. In early 1738, they devised a scheme of building a basin near the quay which would allow access to shipping at all states of the tide and on the 3rd of May they sent the following proposal to Michael Ward:

"We, the owners of the shipping belonging to the port of Killough do propose, provided the Honourable Mr Justice Ward will by the 29th of September 1739, make the pool now called Portaloo into a quay and bason convenient for shipping to load and discharge in and at, as also making a channel from it to the present river in said harbour, a proper breadth and ten foot deep at the lowest tides in winter when smooth water and during the time that the said Mr Justice Ward keep said basin, key and channel in the repair and order before mentioned, we the said owners do promise and engage to and with the said Mr Justice Ward to pay or cause to be paid to him etc., the sum of one penny farthing per ton for

each time any of said ships loads or discharges at or in said harbour, and we further promise to perfect any article pursuant to this proposal for letter securing the said tonnage as witness our hand this day 6th of May 1738".

Signed
William Montgomery Edward Smyth
of Norway

James Feattus	James Keown
Richard West	Thomas Johnston
William Moor	Edward Flin
Samuel Moore	Frances Lascelles

This scheme was duly completed although the finished project consisted of two rather than one basin, one smaller than the other. These can both be seen on a map of Killough made by Alexander Nimmo's in 1820. The name 'Portaloo' seems to have disappeared from both the record and local memory, but the larger basin instead became known as 'Nannie's Sound'. This was located at the rear of what is now known as the Kinder House, while the smaller basin was at the foot of the garden of 38 Castle Street next to the Old Inn. The basins were blocked off sometime between 1820 and 1836 and the Ropewalk was then created as a continuous walkway between the pier and St Anne's Church. Nannie's Sound survived as a hollow for many years after this and Joe McClean of Killough informs me that it was used as a storage area for the masts and spars of sailing ships.

[1]*The present limekiln on the pier was built in 1820 and the site of its predecessor is unknown.*

High Water Mark

Present bottom

Gravel and Clay

Proposed New Cha...

Proposed Addition

Clean Gravel Beach

Dickies Rocks to be cut away

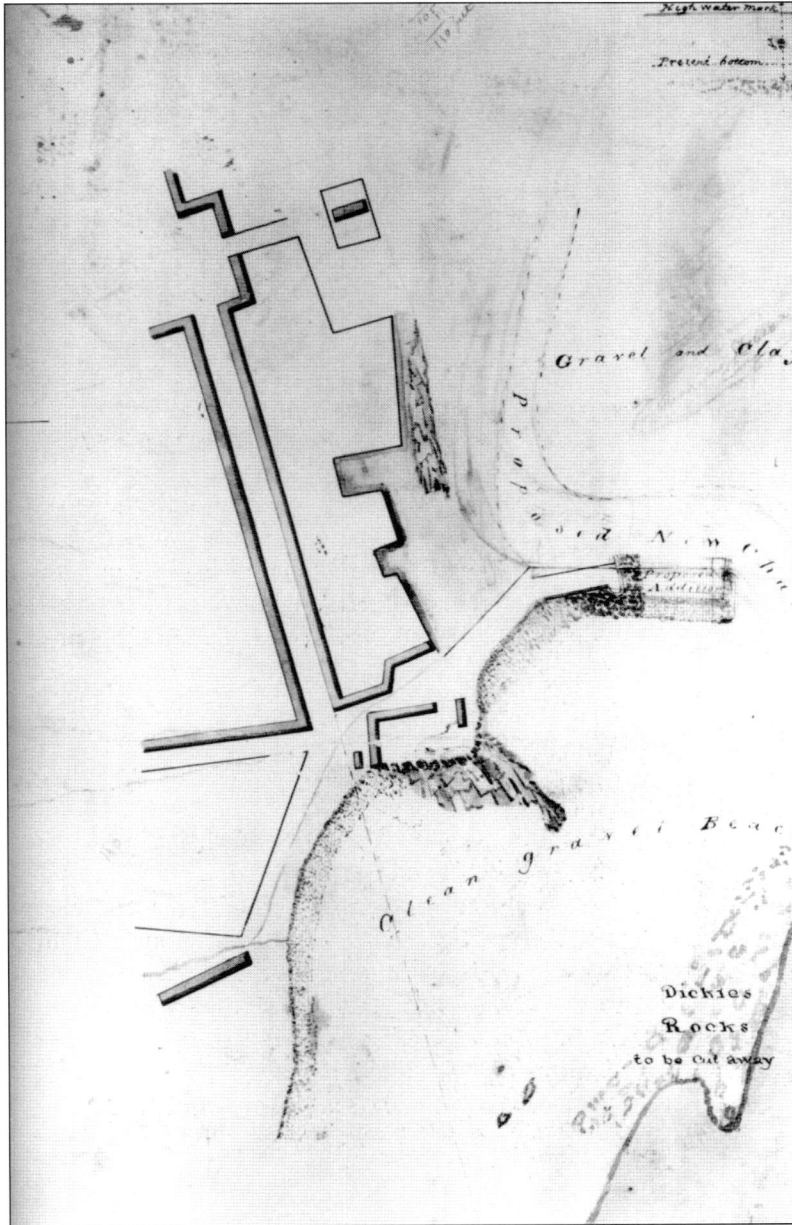

Alexander Nimmo's plan for improved pier 1820 (Courtesy of Down County Museum)

THE EARLY YEARS OF THE PRIMARY SCHOOLS AT KILLOUGH

During the early years of the nineteenth century there were thousands of private primary schools in Ireland ranging from hedge schools to church schools. They were financed by pupil's fees, donations from local landlords, parish funds or by proselytising groups such as the London Hibernian Society or the Baptist Society for Promoting the Bible in Ireland. The government at the time realised that this form of education was of a very piecemeal nature and set up a system of national school education in 1831. The object of the system was to have integrated religious schools, which indeed was already the case in nearly all private schools, but also to have a clear separation between religious and secular teaching. For five days of the week basic numeracy and literacy was to be taught with optional religious teaching by clerics of different denominations on the remaining two days if this was desired. All the churches disliked the system to some degree as they would have liked to

St Joseph's school and church, circa 1920

have seen their interpretation of Christian beliefs taught continually throughout the week in schools.

The Commissioners of National Education, as well as setting up new schools, also incorporated already existing schools into the system. Schools were still fee paying but contributions towards the salaries of teachers, grants of two thirds of any building costs, and running costs such as the part financing of repairs to buildings and the provision of school books all fell within the remit of the new National School Board. The actual management of the schools was left to a group of local trustees, generally led by members of the local clergy and appointees of the local landlord.

A Charter School was built in Killough by Judge Michael Ward in 1737 but this was suppressed in 1772 because of "some charges preferred against the management". It is not until the early nineteenth century that we have further information on schools in Killough. Using funds provided by the Ward estate along with money from the will of the late Rev. Hamilton of Rathmullen a new school was set up in 1828. Additional funds were provided by the London Hibernian Society for the running of the

Palatine Square, circa 1920

school and the payment of its teacher, Mr Robert Nelson, who was also clerk of St Anne's Church. The school was initially located on the site of the Old Barracks in Killough which was situated at the north end of Fisherman's Row. In 1837, the school moved to Palatine Square to a new building provided by Lord Bangor.

In about 1836, the school had some fifty students. It had roughly equal numbers of boys and girls and Catholics and Protestants who all paid one shilling a week for tuition. For some unknown reason, Mr Nelson was sacked from his job in 1840. He responded by setting up his own school in opposition to that of Lord Bangor, after which both schools "were materially injured" and it was only in

1847 that the schools were amalgamated. It is unclear if Robert Nelson continued as teacher but he died in 1857 at the age of 62 and was buried in the graveyard at St. Annes.

In the mid 1830's Mr Nelson's school was only one of four in the village. A Miss Hamilton had a day school for the teaching of needlework and a Mr Smyth ran a 'classical' school. The largest school, with seventy pupils, was taught by a Mr McCartan in his own house. This was again a mixed school of both girls and boys and about three quarters of the students were of the Catholic faith. In 1840, the school was incorporated into the National School system under the clerical sponsorship of Rev. David Whyte and the Rev. John McKenna. At this stage Mr McCartan had been replaced by a Mr Denvir as the teacher in the school and he was provided with an annual salary of £15. With its incorporation into the National School system the numbers of pupils began to increase greatly and in May 1840 it was recorded that there were 143 students in the school although this fell back to 102 within a year. Perhaps they had transferred to Mr Nelson's new breakaway school.

A new building was clearly needed for the school but apparently Lord Bangor, who opposed the school, would not provide a site in the village. The trustees then went into negotiation with a local corn merchant by the name of William Rogan to acquire a long lease on some land on which to build the school. The school, which consisted of two rooms, 24 x 18 feet in size with separate entrances, was subsequently built in late 1841. The commencement of building had been delayed by the fact that the National School Board required a lease of fifty years before they would allocate funds for building works. The two rooms in the school were apparently used for teaching the boys and girls separately. A Mary Keenan was appointed as teacher of the girls school at a salary of £8 but this was increased to £10.6.8 a year later, still significantly less than her male counterpart.

There is little information about the school for several years but in December 31st 1849 we find that Mr Denvir is dismissed for falsifying accounts and despite his appeals for reinstatement he was replaced by a certain Peter Hanlon. The new teacher had immediately to deal with a grave crisis for the school. On the 25th of January the Education Board received from Lord Bangor's Agent, Mr Despard, a message that the school was liable for two years arrears in rent. It transpired that Mr Rogan had granted the long lease on the land for the school for a once off payment of £30 and had agreed that there would be no further annual rent on the property. William Rogan, however, did not have outright ownership of the land and properties in his possession and they were, in fact, leased from Lord Bangor. Unfortunately Rogan's business had failed and he was two years in arrears when Lord Bangor took him to court and was able to repossess all his properties except for the land on which the school was located. It was as a consequence of this that Mr Despard began to demand money from the Educational Board. He threatened that if the arrears were not paid in cash by March 1st he would proceed with legally repossessing the property.

The Education Board was not impressed with this turn in events and blamed the local trustees for having got themselves into such an unfavourable position. It also transpired that the trustees of the school were theoretically liable for much more than the two year rent arrears. A letter was sent to them by the Board stating that "they were bound by a covenant in the trust deed to pay back the grant to the Commissioners in the event of the building being seized for non-payment of rent". In other words, if the local trustees could not sort out the mess they would be liable to pay back the grant given for the building of the school. This news must have caused many sleepless nights in the village.

The local committee did not possess the money to pay the arrears and the deadline came and went, but by August they were informed that they would have to vacate the building by the end of the month. The committee manager went to Mr Despard "begging of him a request of Lord Bangor to re-consider the matter" but was informed that "Lord Bangor must have the school house, as he did not approve of the National system of education". On the 11th of December the Education Board received a letter from the manager "stating that on the 8th of November by order of the Sheriff that the school was taken into possession and the furniture thrown out on the street".

Luckily another merchant in the village, whose name is not given, came to the rescue and he immediately provided a new building for the school. Additionally, the Board also dropped their demand for the building grant to be repaid. The last entry on Killough National School contained in the records in the Public Record Office of Northern Ireland is on the 15th of June 1851 which states that the Education Board was considering an application for three quarters of the cost of the buying of the property which had two stories and "a garden fit for children to play in".

We do not know if the grant was given nor can we be sure of the location of this, or the earlier schools, with the exception of the Lord Bangor School in Palatine Square. In 1860, the National School was located at the then 37 Castle Street which was at the corner of Castle Street and Quay Lane. On an 1838 map this site was occupied by a grain store owned by Patrick Russell. It seems fair to assume therefore that Mr Russell was the businessman who came to the rescue of the National School in 1850 and provided them with the grainstore which was then converted into a school building.

CHARLES SHEILS AND HIS ALMSHOUSES

Charles Sheils, who is buried in the churchyard of St Anne's, left for Liverpool at an early age and amassed a large fortune, apparently in the grain trade. He was renowned for his good deeds and expended much wealth and energy on helping the poor in the area. An example of his work can be seen from this entry in the Downpatrick Recorder in December 1843:

> We have, on former occasions, noticed with satisfaction the kind attention bestowed upon the poorer classes of his native place, Killough, by Charles Sheils Esq., of Liverpool, in affording them employment, although the profits of the work upon which they are engaged may not be remunerative. We have now the pleasure of stating, that that considerate and benevolent gentleman allows to forty indigent persons in Killough, sums varying from 2s 6d to 5s per week, and occasionally provides them with wearing apparel. He has also in the kindest manner, ordered four or five hundred pounds of beef to be provided for the poor of the place at Christmas. These good deeds speak for themselves. They should act as an incentive to others who possess the means of showing practical kindness to their fellow men.

His most enduring legacy, however, came after his death in 1861 with the founding of his almshouses, the first of which was built in Killough. Sheils' will was so complicated that it needed three years and the necessity of converting it into an Act of Parliament to sort it out. The will was duly unveiled as 'An act for Charles Sheils' Almshouses Charity' on the 25th of July 1864.

The will states that all his wealth, most of which was in English railway shares and hotel stock, was to be used in this scheme. He obviously spent an immense amount of time thinking about the project during his latter years and his will contains detailed instructions about how the almshouse should be built and run. He had already before his death negotiated the acquisition of the site in Killough from the Bangor Estate of Castleward. Each almshouse was to be built in "a neat, permanent, and workmanlike manner, with two floors, the ground floor to be raised at least one foot above the level of the adjacent ground, and to contain a sitting room and a kitchen, with scullery, and to contain a place for coal and potatoes, and cupboards, shelves, and other suitable conveniences, with a yard, midden, pighouse and privy in the rear, the upper floor to contain two bedrooms, one a little larger than the other".

Having dealt with the buildings he then moved on to the furniture. Each bedroom was to contain "one good-sized bed and other suitable furniture… with a good strong table and four strong chairs for the sitting room, also a good dresser, with strong drawers underneath, so as to leave no excuse for want of tidiness, or for things lying about in a slovenly manner, also an iron bedstead and neat

Birth Place of Charles Sheils, Castle Street

and in order to give fresh air to the dwellings, all the windows of their bedrooms shall be kept open during a considerable part of every fair day. The privies and middens (kitchen refuse) to be all emptied and cleaned once in every month, and the contents if possible, to be deposited in a proper place, and to be from time to time sold for the benefit of the inmates". Prior to the development for modern chemical fertilizers there was always a ready market for good old fashioned organic manure!

The will states that dogs could only be kept with permission of the manager - there is no mention of cats. Pigs had to be confined to the pigsties and "no pig, horse, cow, ass or goat, or other such animal, to be lodged or even received into any of the almshouses or ornamental grounds". A special area was designated for drying the washing and "no clothes shall be dried or exposed in front of the houses". Poultry too were banned from this area although the implication is that they could be kept around the back.

After a long list of thirty rules for the houses Sheils then turned his mind to the sleeping arrangements in each house under the snappy heading. "Conditions of all the perspective occupants of all the almhouses at any one period of time, and in which scheme, by any words descriptive of children, sons, daughters, nephews, or nieces respectively, I mean to include also grandchildren, grandsons, grand-daughters, grand-

small fireplace for each bedroom, and also a good strong coverlet for each bed, such as will bear scouring in every change of tenant".

He then moves on to who should be allowed admission to the almshouses and states immediately that they should be chosen without reference to religious creed. The almshouses were for the poor of the area who must have lived in or within three miles of Killough during the previous three years. Not only were they to be accommodated but they were also to provided with an annual income.

Sheils then goes into great detail about how the houses should be run giving great attention to detail "all the floors of each house to be thoroughly scrubbed and cleaned at least once in every month, nephews, or grand-nieces respectively". He then went on to produce a convoluted list of who should sleep in each bedroom! A few examples will suffice:

House No. 1. In first bedroom, a man and wife. In second bedroom, the children of the above, not exceeding three, all of one sex.

House No 2. In first bedroom, a man and his wife, with no child. In second bedroom, one widow, with or without a daughter, or two daughters to sleep with her.

House No. 5. In first bedroom, a man, with or without one son of his own or his sister's to sleep with him. In the second bedroom, a sister of the above, a widow, with two of her or her brother's daughters.

It is quite clear that most of these rules disappeared sometime between 1864 and today although theoretically, at least, it could have needed an Act of Parliament to repeal each rule. The original Sheil's Almhouses in Killough were designed by Lanyon who was also responsible for the main building at the Queen's University of Belfast. A further group of houses were added in the early years of the 20th century. They are still in use and play a very important role in providing housing for the community in Killough.

*St Anne's Parish Church,
circa 1940*

THE KILLOUGH LIFEBOAT

A lifeboat committee was based in Killough between 1899 and 1914. The minute book is still preserved in the village and it allows us to follow the career of this gallant group of men who set about making the coast of Co. Down a safer place for shipping.

I

During much of the nineteenth century the lifeboat for Dundrum Bay was located at Tyrella. In the final years of the century the shortage of willing lifeboat men necessitated the setting up of a new committee based at Killough. The inaugural meeting was held on the 3rd of November 1889 in the Viscount Bangor Schoolhouse, Palatine Square, Killough "for the purpose of appointing a local committee in connection with a branch of the Royal National Lifeboat Institution which it has been determined to establish in Killough". Killough was an unsuitable location for the lifeboat as it was too far from Dundrum Bay. It was envisaged that an already

Sailing in Killough Bay by Johnnie McSherry, circa 1890

existing boathouse in Rossglass, some three miles from the village, would be used for the purpose. The minutes of the meeting record that there was a "large attendance of the leading residents of the district, and of principal fishermen of Killough and Rossglass". A Mr Basil Hall, Inspector of Lifeboats explained to the gathered multitude the aims of the project and explained meeting procedures and how a committee should be appointed. The committee was then set up. Lord Bangor was appointed president and predictably took no further part in its doings. Rev. James O'Flaherty, the Minister of St Anne's Killough, was appointed chairman and Mr C. Russell Kelly was appointed Hon. Secretary. The committee was as follows:

Rev. Jas. O'Flaherty	Killough
Mr E. G. Henessy	Dundrum
Rev. Brennan P.P.	Killough
Mr Richard Hughes	Ardglass
Mr J. Donnelly	Ardglass
Mr C. Russell Kelly	Killough
Mr Thos. Mafee	Killough
Mr Alex Moore	Ardglass
Mr Wm. Hannah	Killough
Mr Fran. Murphy	Killough
Mr Gerald Reere	Bright
Mr G. Sampson	Ardglass
Mr. E.W. Browne	Janesville
Mr Henry (Harry) Shanks	Killough
Mr Hugh Finley	Killough

Caption for Map of Killough, 1713. PRONI D/642/G/1

THE HAUEN of PORT Sᵗ ANNᵉ alias KILLOGH in the County of DOWN in the KINGDOM of IRELAND Surveyed and Drawn for Michael Ward Esqʳ by Iohn Sloane Anᵒ 1713

Mr Rob Woods	Ballycam
Dr·Arthur McComiskey	Killough
Mr S.B. Martin	Killough
Dr S. Parkinson- Cumine	Killough
Mr Nath. Hunter	Ardglass
Mr W. Burton	Killough
Mr Thos. Croker	Killough

It took a further two years to set up the project. By November 1901 most of the organisation was in place and at a meeting on the first of that month a crew for the lifeboat was selected. Daniel O'Prey was elected the coxswain and Edward Clarke the assistant coxswain. A Mr Brennan and Mr Harris were selected as signalmen. Mr Basil Hall was again at hand to outline the duties of the different officers and described the need to arrange that six horses be made available for lifeboat practices and life-saving purposes.

A further meeting was held on the 5th of November and it was recorded that the carriage for the lifeboat had arrived and was stored in the lifeboat house at Rossglass. The lifeboat was on passage to Belfast and was expected in Killough by the end of the week. It was to be brought by rail to the village in the charge of Daniel O'Prey and four of the crew. Records show that the Clyde Shipping Co. was paid £9-10-4 for bringing the boat to Belfast while the rail charges amounted to £3-16-9. It was to be rowed from Killough to the boathouse in Rossglass and the committee was confident that they would be able to get volunteers on the day to help with the rowing. Rev. O'Flaherty then went through the rules of the RNLI with the committee so that all would be sure of what they were doing. Launchers were needed and it was decided that a notice would be placed at the boathouses, in

Ardglass and in Killough "asking those willing to undertake the duties to give in their names". The regulations seemed to indicate that two lifeboat crews needed to be recruited but there was some uncertainty in the committee's mind about this so they "deferred action until the inspector for the district could be consulted". Word was also to be sent out to Gun's Island and other coastguard stations to prepare for the reception of the new boat.

The next meeting was held in the loft of the boathouse on December 6th and present for the occasion was the District Inspector of Lifeboats, H. W. Pullan. He stated that he foresaw difficulties in managing the lifeboat with two independent lifeboat crews as had been envisaged at the previous meeting. He stated that in other stations which had a "lengthy crew roll those first ready for service were employed but that [the] coxswain should have a certain right of selection" and that this might be acceptable as a model. Mr Pullan seems to have been taking a gentle approach to the new station and committee and he enquired whether any members of the crew had any experience of the "recommended treatment of persons apparently drowned or suffering from immersion in water". The Hon. Sec. admitted that they had no special knowledge of the subject but that they would ask Dr McComisky to give them some instruction "in case of emergency"!

The following day the crew undertook lifeboat exercises under the scrutiny of Mr Pullan. The boat was launched at low water into a very strong SSW breeze. While generally satisfied with the crew, he notes in the Lifeboat Inspectors' Visiting Book that the crew were "not all to talk and give orders - that remains with the coxswain". He also noted that there had been "considerable difficulty with launching and hauling her up". Clearly discipline was a problem or else the coxswain, Daniel O'Prey, was not providing sufficient leadership. Mr Pullan also ordered some equipment from London which included fifteen oilskins, one dozen each of white, green and red flares and thirty badges for the launchers. Articles to be provided locally were linseed oil for the wires in the lifeboat and a new pin for the roller skid.

A few weeks later, on January 23rd 1902, another exercise was undertaken at which were present not only Mr Pullan but also the Deputy Chief Inspector of Boats, Captain Cunningham-Graham. The launch took only twenty-two minutes despite the carriage getting stuck and the "boat was skidded the remainder of the way" to the water. The crew worked "very satisfactorily" according to the report and it was recommended that 'Tipping's plates' be supplied for the carriage to reduce its chances of being stuck. A meeting with the committee was then held and Captain Cunningham-Graham "expressed his satisfaction at the interest which seems to be taken by the committee and others in this meritous institution" and he hoped that not only would the Killough station become permanent but that it might even undergo expansion! The Hon. Sec. noted that a subscriber's meeting, which elected the committee, had yet to be convened and enquired if it were possible to postpone it for a year and let the committee continue in its present form. He was informed, however, that under RNLI rules this meeting was indeed necessary.

Boats at pier, circa 1920

A meeting of the subscribers was hastily convened five days later in which the present officers were re-elected and the committee remained unchanged except for the addition of Clarence Craig and the substitution of Rev. John Shane P.P. who replaced the deceased Rev Geoffry Brennan. A statement of the finances was read out and the meeting dispersed. The Killough Lifeboat Service was now up an running and ready for action.

II

There were to be four exercises of the Killough lifeboat each year. While generally held at Rossglass there was provision made for horses to be available to bring the boat to Killough for "service or practice". In a report on January 23rd 1902 the District Inspector orders that the following work be undertaken: "Road to Scordon [near Killough] to be widened as necessary" presumably so that the carriage and boat could be brought there for launching. The harbour at Killough was useless for this purpose as boats could only be launched at high tide. Two of the quarterly practices were to be supervised by the local District Inspector and a committee meeting was to be convened to coincide with this.

The supervised exercise on June 11th 1902 started routinely with a launch at "one hours flood" and all seems to have gone favourably until the boat came back to land. The minutes record "On his [District Inspector Mr Pullan] return to the beach he was informed by Hon. Sec. that the launchers had struck for increased pay". Their argument was that only twenty launchers were employed instead of the thirty that were theoretically necessary. Instead of the usual two shillings pay they consequently wanted 3/- to compensate for the extra work they were doing. Mr Pullan was clearly not impressed and informed them that the rules of the RNLI stated that the fee for 'summer' launches was fixed at 2/- and reminded them that because of the condition of the tide that the "work to be done was much lighter than if launch had been about time of low water". He had been compromised in his argument, however, because the Hon. Sec. C. Russell Kelly had already offered them 2/6 when he had been out on manoeuvres with the crew. He therefore had to confirm the new offer, although he knew that it was technically against rules, but the launchers refused the compromise payment and stuck to their demand for the 3/-.

Mr Pullan then demanded that the launchers return their badges and informed them that they were getting no pay whatsoever for the day. All excepting two returned the badges and the strikers seemed to have looked on as Mr Pullan, the crew, helped by committee members Messrs. Shanks, Griffin and Upstall, put the boat on the carriage, "with some difficulty" according to Mr Pullan's report, and hauled it back into the boat house. Mr Pullan then further annoyed the striking launchers by awarding the crew members an extra 2/-, i.e. the equivalent of a launchers fee, for their "uncommonly hard" work and gave the two launchers that did not go on strike 2/6 for their troubles. One wonders how these arbitrary payments squared with the RNLI rules that had been so strongly quoted earlier in the day.

At any rate, tempers amongst the striking launchers must have been high as Mr Pullan again reiterated his judgement that they get no pay

NO **C** 19
Royal National Life-Boat Institution

KILLOUGH BRANCH.

Nov 25. 1905

A Brereton Martin

	£	s.	d.
Annual Subscrip- *tion,* 1905......		5/	—
Donation			
Life Donation			
£		5/	—

Killough Lifeboat Receipts

bitterness in minds of men it might be desirable to pay them 1/- each for what they had done". The committee accepted this compromise. Mr Pullan's feelings are unclear but at the meeting he praised the work of the crew during the exercise, thanked the committee for helping get the boat out of the water, and expressed satisfaction with the condition of the boathouse. Before he left, however, he noted that there was "poor spelling" on the notice-board on the door of the lifeboat station and ordered that it be taken down and the names of the Hon. Sec. and coxswain's be added to it before it was re-erected. The cash book records that the correcting of the notice-board by a painter cost 1/-.

Mr Pullan's days were numbered as he died suddenly between this inspection and the winter. He seems to have been a very popular person with the committee as the first resolution passed on the December 10th meeting was that an expression of sympathy be passed to his widow and it recorded its "fullest approval of his conduct when connected with the committee". His duties at that practice were taken by a Comt. Thomas Holmes and he introduced the new District Inspector, Lieut. P. Maclean to the committee. The row with the launchers seems to have been forgotten about because the Inspector noted that the experienced crew and launchers had "all worked satisfactorily and pleasantly". The boat had been launched at low tide and this had been accomplished in twenty minutes. The 'Tippings plates' which had been fixed to the wheels were "found most efficient on soft part of the beach where wheels had previously sunk". Some pieces of equipment were found to be unsuitable and it was decided to return them to the Lifeboat headquarters in London. These included "horse launching poles and gear". The reason why

because of the refusal to have completed their designated tasks that day. The Hon. Sec. tried to defuse the situation by pointing out to the district inspector that the launchers, because of their low numbers "really had a stiff job" during the earlier part of the days exercise. They had hauled the carriage up to the road, had "done the usual oiling of wheels and rollers and prepared the hauling up gear before the strike" and he argued that "while fully agreeing that their conduct was very bad and most unjustifiable" that "in view of the possibility of working the station in the future and to remove there was no mention of the launchers row can be found in the cash book for the station which shows that the launchers had been paid 3/- for the day's work.

The previous years Subscribers Meeting had been a rather perfunctory affair merely rubber-stamping the existing committee and generally ignoring the financial affairs of the station. The March 3rd meeting of 1903 was much more detailed. It was found that subscriptions, donations and collection boxes had contributed £26-9-5 for

Sailing boat in Killough Bay

the year but the actual running costs were nearly twice that much at £49-9-1. The accounts show that the balance was made up of monies from London.

The next meeting on April the 24th was generally routine. A letter of thanks from Mrs Pullan was read for the sympathy that was sent to her. Specific troubles in launching the boat were now being addressed. The door of the boathouse had been widened by 2 feet since the last launch and P. Maclean's report records that there was now "no difficulty in getting the boat in and out". In the previous February, 4/- had been spent on levelling the beach again, presumably, to facilitate launching. The launch on the 24th had taken place in light wind and smooth water and the crew were found to be satisfactory. It was, however, noted that the "hauling up of the boat and replacing on carriage and in boathouse was tedious mainly owing to bad condition of upper part of shore and narrowness of road and the bad position necessary for turntable".

III

Mr Maclean made a surprise visit to Killough a month later (May 27th) and found the boathouse in good order. He convened a meeting with some of the committee to come to a conclusion "on the best means of getting boat up and into the [boat] house". A report on their deliberations were sent to London. In July, Mr Maclean arranged for the boat to be brought to "Port Scordon" in Killough for an exercise but the conveyance of the lifeboat was not satisfactory. The account book notes that 7/6 was spent on "cleaning of road for Killough launch" and in his report Maclean states that "It is not advisable except under most perfect conditions to get through by road - or in extreme emergency".

Maclean did not meet the committee on that occasion and it is not until the meeting of December 15th that we get more information about the proposed improvements for access to the boathouse at Rossglass. We learn that the Honorary Secretary Mr C. Russell Kelly had been "directed to see tenant of farm adjoining County road at launching beach in Rossglass with view to arranging for possession of portion of his field to facilitate hauling up of lifeboat and had offered him £10 for the desired plot but [the] tenant held to £20 which was considered excessive". On the day of the meeting the Hon. Sec. and the inspector had again gone to the tenant in the hope of acquiring the plot but "failed to move him to any concessions". They also walked and examined the beach to see if there was any alternative place where launching could be arranged but concluded that there was none. Mr Maclean decided that the Lifeboat Institution might feel it necessary to pay the high price asked "to secure against accidents for launchers or lifeboat when hauling up the latter". The Hon. Sec. was asked to write to the agent of the tenant's landlord to see if he could consent to the sale of the land. The exercise on the day went satisfactorily but he asked that the committee "get [the] windows of the boathouse to work" and he ordered equipment from headquarters in London including a hammer, screwdriver, and a tin of lubricating oil.

The next exercise on March 14th 1904 was not as successful as the previous outings. The main problem was that someone had removed the "Tipping plates" from the wheels of the carriage, and this along with the state of the tide led to the carriage getting stuck in the dreaded "sand at soft point of beach". The exercise was held in a light breeze but there was "trouble and delay in getting carriage and boat hauled back to firmer ground" when again going over the soft ground. One of the crew became "very offensive in his remarks on the occurrence". Mr Maclean recommended that the "Tipping plates be never taken off [the] carriage for launching at Rossglass". The required land had been bought since the last meeting and the inspector "reported that the new arrangement for hauling up had proved very convenient and seemed to fully justify the expense incurred for ground and fittings and the work which was nearly completed seemed in all respects to be satisfactory". Materials ordered from London included paint for boat, wheels and boathouse and twelve red cartridges. The accounts later record that it cost 30/- to have the boat painted.

There was no annual subscribers meetings in 1904 and the committee elected in March 1903 seems to have continued in place but the active committee members had shrunk to a few reliables. C. Russell Kelly, the Hon. Sec. was always present as was generally Rev. James O'Flaherty the Chairman. General Browne of Janesville was also a regular attendant as was Harry Shanks, Mr Upstall, Hugh Finley. P. Maclean, the District Inspector, was also invariably present. Most meetings consisted of only four to six people and it seems the concept of a quorum was not considered. The meeting on September 1st 1904 is unusual in that the Hon. Sec. received a wire from Viscount Bangor expressing his inability to attend, although he had not attended any meeting since the inaugural one five years before. He was probably just reminding them that he was still President of the branch.

Apathy was also beginning to develop on the part of the launchers, and poor relations were beginning to arise between the coxswain, Daniel O'Prey and the District Inspector. Inspector Maclean noted that the hauling up of the boat had been "tedious and troublesome mainly owing to insufficient attendance of launchers only seventeen having attended instead of thirty and they too were of too juvenile a type in many cases". It was thought that the demands of the harvest contributed mainly to the low attendance level. Not only were the launchers deficient but Mr Maclean also reported that "he regretted to say that he had to complain to coxswain of what he considered the untidy nature of the boathouse floor which had needed sweeping out and the coxswain had replied in an unbecoming manner and told him he was by his carping and fault-finding driving the best men from serving in crew and soon none would come frequently … when he attended". The minutes continue "the District Inspector desired that this matter be examined with a view to efficiency of station" and had ordered that the coxswain attend the committee meeting after the exercise.

The coxswain in reply to inquiry said he considered that the Inspector was "too particular with him and crew" and that the mess on the boathouse floor had been caused "by trampling of [the] public with dirty boots upon opening of door that forenoon before Inspector's arrival". The committee was clearly unimpressed with coxswain O'Prey's defence and C. Russel Kelly's minutes continues "he was cautioned by chairman and some members of the committee about his future conduct and after some further conversation the matter was dropped". While this meeting had being going on the crew and launchers had been left unsupervised to haul up the boat and get it back into the boathouse. Because of their limited numbers they now demanded further remuneration for their work. A quick and uncontested decision seems to have been made and the money that would have been due to the thirteen launchers that had not attended was distributed amongst those present with all receiving ten pence extra for their troubles. Before the meeting dispersed the Hon Sec. said that in future he would avoid a clash with the harvest when arranging the summer exercise.

On February 27th 1905 the lifeboat held an exercise in a full half gale from SSW and a considerable sea. In Mr Maclean's report he notes that "boat behaved splendidly and crew [were] very pleased with boat". He reported that the lifeboat was exercised "for a time under full sail and he had instructed the coxswain to let her feel the strength of it. He could not put her rail under water and she had worked well in all conditions. He then had two reefs tied in an exercise for crew and she had then behaved equally well". For once "the hauling up of boat had been done satisfactorily". He then noted that in "several stations lists of three or four crews were regularly enrolled and each was called on in turn for quarterly practice and each member detailed for his special work which tended to greater efficiency" and suggested that this could well be accomplished at the present station. Clearly on this occasion the Inspector and crew were working in harmony, satisfied with the fact that they had been so successful in the most difficult conditions as yet encountered in an exercise.

IV

General Brown of Janesville was a person who regarded life-saving in the area as a matter of family

91

pride. His ancestors had organised a private lifeboat service in the early nineteenth century and had agitated greatly for the building of the Lighthouse at John's Point. His forebearers too had been instrumental in the setting up of the lifeboat station at Tyrella. An incident on the 15th of March 1905 annoyed him greatly in that he felt that the Killough lifeboat branch had not performed its duty in the case of a rescue. He wrote to the Hon. Sec. demanding a special meeting in order to set up a sub-committee to examine the said incident. Those present at the meeting on the 2nd of March were C. Russell Kelly, Rev. O'Flaherty, Harry Shanks, Dr McComisky, Hugh Finley, J.C. Upstall, Richard Hughes and, of course, General Browne.

General Brown demanded to know why the boat was not launched from Rossglass on the 15th between the hours of noon and 10pm. Clearly implying that the branch was inefficient and ineffective, he also wanted to "organise a system for the assembling at Rossglass of crew any time when a vessel seemed in danger that it may be ready for immediate action when practicable". He also wanted the sub-committee to "enquire into Coastguard's duty in an emergency and whether this were discharged in recent case". Clearly, General Browne thought that the organisation of life saving activities in the area would be better under his supervision than in the hands of the local RNLI branch or the Coastguards.

The situation on the day in question was, as recorded by C. Russell Kelly, as follows; "Soon after 10 a.m. on the 15th the Coast Guard reported a barque had passed Annalong with spint sails but no distress signal and he directed the coxswain who was in attendance to have launchers and crew in readiness and to keep watch for vessel and render aid if necessary. He had no further intimation of help being needed till 5 o'clock when signalman brought him message from the Coast Guard officer

Wreck of the Coeur de Lion, Dundrum Bay, in 1828 by Leslie Jones (1999)

at Newcastle that their lifeboat was ashore at Tyrella and suggesting that ours be sent by road to Dundrum for service. That from [his] experience of road-work and knowledge of road he felt it was impossible to effect this and from force and direction of wind which had westerned and on consultation with coxswain and signalman he considered launching at Rossglass most dangerous for boat and crew and that he would not be justified in attempting it and directed reply to Newcastle to this effect and when practicable boat would proceed by sea unless countermanded". He further stated that "he had message at 10 o'clock from Newcastle that rescue had then been affected by … Newcastle lifeboat". The coxswain was also present at the meeting and he stated "that crew was ready but owing to wind and sea at the time he could not have launched boat and taken her to sufficient offing for setting sail and proceeding to sea and Mr Upstall, Coastguard Officer, expressed same opinion".

Ship's figureheads used as garden ornaments at Minerstown circa 1880. (Courtesy of Down Museum)

General Brown was not convinced with this version of the day and proposed that Hugh Finley and Harry Shanks should make an enquiry into the affair. This was seconded by Richard Hughes who added that Dr McComiskey and the Hon. Sec. should be on this sub-committee of enquiry. If five of these persons were in favour of an enquiry they would have constituted a majority of those present and forced the issue through. C. Russell Kelly, the Hon. Sec., was clearly against the motion and said he would refuse to partake in the investigation stating "he considered it a matter reflecting his own action". He therefore had managed to present the issue as one of accepting or rejecting his judgement on the day of the incident. With the matter becoming personalised in this way Richard Hughes withdrew his seconding of the motion and with this General Browne's scheme collapsed. Just in case there was any doubt as to who had won this battle between Browne and Russell Kelly, the Hon. Sec. then read a letter he had prepared on the previous Monday accepting full responsibility for not launching the lifeboat on the day in question. The committee then voted and accepted that they "approved of action of Hon. Sec. and of crew and had full confidence in them". General Browne abstained from this vote.

One further outcome of that disputed day emerged in the next meeting on December the 18th 1905. The crew and launchers had not been paid because the lifeboat had not actually been launched and the committee brought this anomaly to the attention of the District Inspector. He voiced the opinion that "in the event of crew and launchers being assembled for service no doubt the Institution on a representation of the circumstances would sanction a payment to them for such assembly". The exercise on the same day, in a "strong breeze and high sea", was successful as was the state of the boathouse, the only task being necessary was the that the "gravel outside the boathouse [was] to be scuffed".

The meeting of July 3rd 1906 recorded that Edward Clarke, the assistant coxswain, had recently been drowned. The District Inspector stated that it was customary to consult the crew before any appointment was made. He had spoken to them about it during the afternoon exercise but as some of the regular crew were absent herring fishing, a final decision could not be made. In the meantime a temporary appointment of Patrick Burns who had previously worked as bowman was made to fill the vacancy, and the William Maginnis be made a temporary bowman.

V

On August 2nd the lifeboat got called to its first service. At 6.05 a.m. John Rogan and a Coastguard had reported to the Hon. Sec. C. Russel Kelly that a steamer had gone ashore at Corely point to the west of St John's Lighthouse and that nothing was known of the crew. By order of Hon. Sec. the assembly gun was fired and the lifeboat was launched before 7 a.m. into a moderate SSE wind. They proceeded by row alongside the steamer which by now had the sea heavily breaking over it. There was no crew aboard as they had managed to get ashore on their own boats. The lifeboat was back in the boathouse by 8 o'clock. The steamer was the Cuer SS of Chester and it was carrying about 200 tons of coal from Burghfort to Portaferry. It had run aground about 1 a.m. in dense fog. The crew of seven left the ship into a rising tide but remained attached to the ship until about 5.30 a.m, when the fog lifted and they were able to land. They had been taking shelter in the lighthouse when the Killough lifeboat went to the rescue. The accident report noted that the boat would probably be a total wreck and we are not told if it was re-floated. None of crew of the lifeboat had ever been in a rescue before and this, their first, was a pretty undramatic affair. The crew consisted of Daniel O'Prey (Cox), William Magennis, Rob Magennis, Alex O'Prey, John McCullough, Thomas Digney, Rob Taylor, James Doran, John McMullan, William J. Burns, Patrick Burns, Bernard O'Prey, John Rogan and William Cochrane.

Because the crew had seen action there was no need for the quarterly exercise but at the meeting of the committee on September 12th the temporary positions for assistant cox and bowman were confirmed as permanent. It was also noted that the road next to the boat-house was being broken away by wave action. The Hon. Sec. was directed to contact the council about this so that it could be secured. At the next meeting on February 22nd 1907 it was noted that the council had promised to implement repairs in the coming Spring.

For some reason there was no further supervised exercise or committee meeting in the summer of 1907 but the lifeboat was once again called into service on November 4th. At about 3 a.m. in the morning, some seven miles South East of St John's point, the three masted schooner Ester of Fleetwood lost her foremast and main topmast in a strong southerly breeze. She was travelling from Falmouth to Glasgow with a cargo of 234 tons of Cornish china clay and a crew of five. At 8 o'clock in the morning she was spotted by the Coastguard with only mizen and main mast standing heading in a northerly direction under mizen sail alone. The lifeboat was launched before 9 o'clock and proceeded to her under oars to offer help. They left two of the crew on board and returned to shore, only to have the captain contact them and request that they come back alongside until a tug that had been summoned had arrived and towed them to safety. When the tug, owned by a Mr McCauseland, arrived, the lifeboat again went ashore but two of the crew, Pat Burns and Bernard O'Prey, remained with the vessel at the captain's request, until she safely berthed at Portaferry for repairs. The lifeboat arrived ashore at 2.45 p.m. and was safely back in the boathouse by 3.15 p.m. Many of the crew had already been out on the previous rescue but for some, this was their first taste of action, i.e. Pat Burns (assistant cox), Henry Taylor, William Small, Patrick McKevitt, Henry Ward, Patrick Henvey and Henry Armstrong.

The next meeting was on January 3rd 1908 and was for the most part concerned with improving the landing strip. The county council had repaired the road and the London board had sent them £20 for other improvements but they considered this too little money and that "nothing permanent could be done for that amount". Harry Shanks informed the group that "for £40 he would construct a slip 60 x 40 feet or thereabouts of stones pitched on end 12" x 18" in depth and grouted with good strong concrete to depth of about 10", which he believed would be effective for desired purpose". The committee agreed to "recommend this course of procedure". London accepted the recommendation and the slipway was built by the said Shanks. An unscheduled meeting was convened on May 13th to check the work and they "approved of the manner in which it had been carried out".

At the quarterly exercise and meeting on June 19th, the District Inspector noted that the "new concrete gangway appears satisfactory" but noted that "he had been told there was a danger of abrasion by [the] sea to a short wing of the beach between south side of slip and boathouse and suggested it might be desirable to have this part fitted with stone and cement". This might have been seen as an oblique criticism of Harry Shanks work because the Chairman, Dr McComisky, seconded by Harry Shanks, proposed instead that "this need not be asked for until action of sea during coming winter will have been experienced". District Inspector Maclean suggested the acquisition of a winch such as had been supplied to other stations could be installed and that it would be "found convenient and desirable for speedy launching and hauling up". He also noted that the "handling rope should soon be renewed" and it was agreed for this.

There had been no road exercise of the lifeboat since the trip to Scordon in July 1903 and the District Inspector desired that there should be another. Unfortunately, it had been found impossible to obtain horses for the purpose. Mr

Ketch Mary-Ann leaving Killough about 1825 by Leslie Jones

Hugh Finley, seconded by Mr Henry Pyne, proposed that "consequent on narrow conditions of our roads, the severe difficulty, amounting almost to impossibility, of suitable horses in this district for team drawing, and remembering the slow progress under most favourable circumstances when boat was brought by road to Killough in summer of 1903, the local committee is strongly of the opinion that road exercise should be dispersed with at this station". The District Inspector was clearly not getting his way!

At the next meeting on November 9th 1908 the Hon. Sec. was able to report that London had agreed to dispense with road exercises due to the special circumstances and they had agreed to supply the winch but that it had not yet arrived. He also stated that when the assembly gun had been fired for the July 19th exercise, the crew turned up but only twelve of the launchers had arrived and it had not been able to launch the boat. He had reported this to London and they had directed that 2/- each be paid to the launchers who had responded to the signal and 6d extra to the crew. District Inspector Maclean stated that he was much disappointed that the winch had not arrived and that he would write to London to state that if it was not promptly sent they should dispatch a new launching rope worth £20 as the present one was becoming unusable. A bilge bearer on the carriage had been accidentally broken during the last unsupervised exercise on August 20th and had been repaired at a cost of 20/-. This accident had been caused by the insecure fastening of a rope or chain securing the boat to the carriage and the District Inspector had cautioned the coxswain about this so that the accident would not be repeated. Since there was to be no more road exercises the committee proposed that all the horse harness fittings should be returned to London.

VI

A third rescue mission of the branch occurred on the 29th of December 1908, when the passenger ship S.S. Galteemore ran into a SE gale. At about 6.30 in the morning, a phone call from Newcastle alerted the Coastguard that the ship had run aground between Newcastle and Tyrella and that the Newcastle lifeboat could not be launched. Assembly was first at Killough and the boat was launched at about 8 o'clock into a very heavy sea and proceeded across the bay almost to Newcastle without seeing any vessel there or homeward.

The report continues "when in view of St. John's Lighthouse again, went westwards and met large steamer near shore off Ringmore rocks at Tyrella and boarded on her. She proved to be the Galteemore with passengers and cargo from Holyhead to Greenore and did not know [its] position owing to thickness shorewards. They got particulars from the lifeboat and then proceeded and lifeboat then returned to station. But for information given the steamer might have gone ashore as water was shoal where she was. The service was excellent as the weather was very bad with SE gale and heavy sea and rain and it was bitterly cold". The report then notes that "the boat was well tried and worked well though at times was almost filled by the heavy seas". All the rescue was undertaken under sail and on returning "when near station the centreboard was found jammed and for a time would not come up and [the] boat lashed [with] some of crew getting knocked about in her. Coxswain went overboard to

St. John's Point Lighthouse,
CO. DOWN.

9th August, 1950.

Engineer,
Irish Lights Office,
DUBLIN.

Sir,

I have to report the painter B. Behan absent from his work all day yesterday and not returning to station until 1.25 a.m. this morning. No work has been carried out by him yesterday (Tuesday). I also have to report that his attitude here is one of careless indifference and no respect for Commissioners' property or stores. He is wilfully wasting materials, opening drums and paint tins by blows from a heavy hammer, spilling the contents which is now running out of the paint store door. Drums of water-wash opened and exposed to the weather — paint brushes dirty and lying all round the station — no cleaning up of any mess but he tramps through everything. His language is filthy and he is not amenable to any law or order.

He has ruined the wall surface of one wall in No. 1 Dwelling by burning. He mixes putty, paint, etc. with his bare hands and wipes off nothing. The spare house which was clean and ready for painters has been turned into a filthy shambles inside a week. Empty stinking milk bottles, articles of food, coal, ashes and other debris litter the floor of the place which is now in a scandalous condition of dirt.

I invite any official of the Irish Lights to inspect this station and verify these statements.

He is the wrost specimen I have met in 30 years service. I urge his dismissal from the job now before good material is rendered useless and the place ruined.

Your obedient Servant,

D. Blakely
Principal Keeper.

The writer Brendan Behan was a painter and decorator by trade. For a while he worked for Irish Lights and while working at St. John's Lighthouse he spent much of his time socialising in Killough. As can be seen in this letter the Principal Keeper was plainly unimpressed with his behaviour.

try and relieve it and got slightly crushed but is little the worse and later centre board was found free and was safely housed". Two of the crew hurt their ankles in the process.

With the exception of this, all were back on shore safely at 1 p.m.

The fifteen crew were as follows; Daniel O'Prey (cox), Patrick Burns (assistant cox), William Maginnis (bowman), Henry McSherry, Bernard O'Prey, John and Henry McKevitt, Patrick McIlmeal, Hugh Cleary, Thomas West, Patrick Burns, Thomas Digney, Samuel Cargill, William Cochrane and James McEvoy.

At the meeting on March 22nd 1909, further deterioration of equipment was noted. A plank in the lifeboat was split and it was suggested that the RNLI Surveyor should visit the station and examine the boat. The good news was that the winch had arrived and worked satisfactorily. The person who worked the winch clearly performed a task that set him aside from the other launchers, so it was proposed that John Rogan be appointed the head launcher and winchman and that he be paid 2/- more than the other launchers on all occasions. The winch was deemed as a great addition to the station and it was proposed that "a wooden cover be made to protect it from the weather". The boat house roof was also beginning to show wear and tear and it was proposed that it be repaired. Some of the old core team in the committee were also suffering from the passing of time. Mr C. Russel Kelly had sent a letter "stating that owing to illness he was unable to continue as Hon. Sec." This news was received "with great regret" and it was decided to send a message of "condolence" to him. When he recovered he continued as a member of the committee but did not resume his former position. Harry Shanks was appointed as acting Hon. Sec. until another was found.

It is quite clear that C. Russel Kelly had been the driving force of the branch and now the whole affair went into swift decline. A permanent Hon. Sec. could not be found among the present committee as all would have been aware of the onerous task that this position entailed.

At a meeting on April 27th a Mr W. Flynn was elected to the committee and made the new Hon. Sec. The August 9th inspection and exercise were satisfactory "with an exception that some large boulders were greatly in the way at the bottom of the slip and that the coxswain be requested to have same removed". It was noted that a new official notice board was to be obtained from London containing the names and addresses of the Hon. Sec., cox and assistant cox, as well as noting where the keys of the boathouse could be obtained.

Inspector Maclean's last exercise and inspection took place on February 19th 1910 and on that instance the affair was rather unsatisfactory. He stated that "he had exercised the boat that day in rough weather and was very disappointed in the way some of the launchers worked and also with a few of the crew. The boat was 1½ hours being got into the water and was 1 hour afloat". The minutes record that a telephone be installed in the 2nd coxswain's house and that he should be asked how much money he would like to be paid so that an estimate could be sent for confirmation to London. The equipment and clothing of the branch also needed servicing. Mr Maclean notes "coxswain during summer months to clean and overhaul oilskins and all ... oily marks to be removed with a solution of 1 oz of soda to one pint of water. A small remuneration to be given to coxswain for work done".

During July a small incident occurred in which some six members of the crew rescued one person in a boat who was being driven out to sea in rough weather. Details are scarce but it seems the lifeboat was not used. A letter from RNLI headquarters at 22 Charing Cross Road, London, congratulated the men on their "services rendered" and gave them an award of 5/- on top of their usual launching fees.

VII

The meeting of the 26th of June 1911 marked the beginning of the end of the Killough branch with the arrival of the new District Inspector, a certain

FOUNDED 1824.

ROYAL NATIONAL LIFE-BOAT INSTITUTION.

(Supported solely by Voluntary Contributions).

Patrons—{ His Majesty the King. / Her Majesty the Queen. / Her Majesty Queen Alexandra.

President—His Grace the Duke of Northumberland, K.G.
Chairman—The Right Hon. the Earl Waldegrave, P.C., V.P.
Deputy-Chairman—Sir John Cameron Lamb, C.B., C.M.G., V.P.
Secretary—George F. Shee, Esq., M.A.

ALL COMMUNICATIONS SHOULD BE ADDRESSED TO THE SECRETARY, ROYAL NATIONAL LIFE-BOAT INSTITUTION.

Telegraphic Address:—
"Life-Boat Institution, London."

Telephone:—
2964. "Gerrard" Exchange.

22, Charing Cross Road, London, W.C.

13th November, 1913.

Dear Sir,

At a Meeting of the Committee of Management held here today, I submitted a report of the District Inspector with regard to the Surprise Exercise which he carried out at midnight on the 17th ultimo, together with his report upon the proceedings at the Meeting of your Committee.

I am instructed to inform you that, in view of the inefficiency of the Coxswain and the crew, it has been decided that the Station should be temporarily closed and a Caretaker appointed.

I am to state that a reasonable time will be allowed within which, it is hoped, that your Committee may procure a suitable Coxswain and a more efficient crew.

The Committee of Management also hope that more assistance will be given by the Local Committee and that

a

-2-

a better supervision will be kept over the Station and crew.

Will you please appoint a satisfactory Caretaker and inform me when he has been appointed.

I am,

Yours faithfully,

Secretary.

William Flynn, Esq.,
Killough.

Letter: Closing of Lifeboat Station, 1913

Lieut. W. Rigg. He was of a totally different character than the amiable Mr Maclean. The reason for the appointment of a new inspector is not, however, explained to us in the surviving records. On his first visit, all seemed well. He did not take the lifeboat out for an exercise, as it had already been out in the water and found all in the station "in good order". He was, however, disappointed with the small turnout of the committee to meet him which consisted only of W. Flynn and Rev. J. O'Flaherty and he asked that a full compliment of members be present for his next visit. He found too that much of the equipment was not up to standard and left some instructions for the crew. Some of these looked rather finicky, and included "blackboard to be hung on wall … axes and hatchets to be ground". He also wanted the winch to be oiled, boathouse to be cleaned down inside, stairs and platform to committee-room to be repaired and bird dung to be cleared away.

Lieut. Rigg returned on November 7th for a meeting with the committee in the Bangor Arms Hotel [presently the Old Inn] but unfortunately there are no minutes of the meeting except to record that Rev. J. O'Flaherty was in the chair. W. Rigg's notes tell us that he exercised the boat for an hour and a half in a SW breeze and all seemed well. The station was in good order although the winch wire still needed oiling, the roadway in front of the boathouse needed to be repaired as did "staircase and railings".

He was back on the 15th and 17th of May 1912 but only to visit the boathouse and there was no exercise or meeting with the committee. He was clearly unhappy with what he found. His report states "Inspected boathouse - the boat was dirty and the fittings of the boat and house generally required attention - ropes should be kept on board the boat - the compliment of hand lights to be kept on board re. 6 red, 4 white and 2 green. The bilges were not chained". Indeed Lieut. Rigg found a multitude of things that were not to his satisfaction and left a long list of instructions. This must have exceedingly annoyed the committee as it entailed a considerable amount of work and organisation. Most of these are of a technical nature pertaining to the boat and carriage. They included such tasks as the "nuts of the carriage to be tightened up by the blacksmith; the bilgeways of the carriage to be lightly dressed down to give one eighth of an inch clearance for bilge keels". Work to slipway was also in order. The slipway needed to be protected by "a trench to be dug and large boulders to be laid in to prevent scour". Rigg was clearly a perfectionist. The axes and hatchets that needed sharpening on the last visit now needed "to be cleaned and coated with falr. solution and the edges with … rust grease"

On his visit on August 12th 1912 Lieut. Rigg recorded that "inspected station and exercised boat. The boat was clean and the house tidier but there is still room for improvement". He noted that many of the tasks set out on his last visit had not been undertaken. He was totally unimpressed with the lifeboat exercise "the crew are lazy and require much attention at exercises. Silence should be maintained and only the coxswain and head launcher should give instructions". Again there was a long list of jobs to be done before his next visit, in addition to completing the instructions from his previous visit. These included "birds nests to be removed from guttering and window of committee room". The committee by this stage seems to have gone into decline. There were very few meetings during 1912 or 1913, and when they were held there were little in the way of records being kept.

Lieut. Rigg then seems to have complained to the headquarters in London and must have suggested that the station should be closed as it was, in his opinion, so badly run. In late October he was back for a special meeting "by order of the committee of management" in order to "organise" the crew. The exercise got off to a bad start as most of the launchers had clearly had enough of Rigg, so only six of them turned up for the work. In most circumstances a launching would be difficult with so few launchers but the fact that the tide was at low water made the launch even more difficult. This, however, did not deter Lieut. Rigg who notes that the boat was launched "plainly showing the men are capable of doing this work if they are willing". On this exercise Daniel O'Prey and John Rogan seem to have become the main focus of his anger because of their failure to exercise control. He records "coxswain must take more charge of the men. The winch man [J. Rogan] must be much more careful in keeping proper control of the boat, otherwise a bad accident is soon to occur".

He seems to have left in a bad temper leaving a note stating that "the Hon. Sec. is requested to get the items marked in the district inspector's report … carried out at once". Finally, and ominously, he warned the crew "A night surprise visit will take place before the end of the year when it will be definitely settled, by the manner in which the work was carried out, if the station shall remain open".

Clearly this threat frightened the crew and committee. A man of his word Lieut. Rigg was down for his surprise night visit on the 27th of December and the exercise seems to have gone reasonably well: "gun was fired at 10 o'clock and the boat was out in fifty minutes. Crew and helpers worked well". Daniel O'Prey was again, however, failing to impress as the report notes "cox was late, being the last man to arrive, except for that the boat would have been in the water quicker". To avoid delays like this in the future Rigg stated "the enrolled crew can only be waited for an hour, after that crew must be filled up". Clearly feeling that more practice was needed he ordered that two more unsupervised exercises must take place before his next surprise visit scheduled for March.

VIII

At this stage most of Mr Rigg's records, as well as the committee minutes are missing, probably because they were not written down in the first place. There is one final report of his on the 9th of August 1913. Again it was a list of complaints: "inspected station and found all in a disgraceful state. The orders left … have not yet been carried out … birds nests are still in the gutters … found all the gear out of the boat and the boat in no way ready for service … all garments to be taken off the oars…"

He had clearly had enough of the station and a surprise visit sometime later did not change his opinion. On the 13th of November 1913 the following letter from RNLI headquarters in London was sent to William Flynn, the Hon. Sec. of the committee.

Dear Sir,
At a meeting of the Committee of Management held here today, I submitted a

report of the District Inspector with regard to the Surprise Exercise which he carried out at midnight on the 17th ultimo, together with his report upon the proceedings at the Meeting of your committee.

I am instructed to inform you that, in view of the inefficiency of the coxswain and the crew, it had been decided that the station should be temporally closed and a Caretaker appointed.

I am to state that a reasonable time will be allowed which, it is hoped, that your committee may procure a suitable Coxswain and a more efficient crew.

The Committee of Management also hope that assistance will be given by the Local Committee and that a better supervision will be kept over the station and crew.

Will you please appoint a satisfactory Caretaker and inform me when he has been appointed.

I am,
Yours faithfully,
F. Shee
Secretary

The end of the Killough lifeboat branch was fast approaching. It seems to have reopened for a time a during 1914 and there were unsuccessful attempts to recruit a crew in Ardglass. A telegram sent from Ardglass to Mr Flynn on January 31st contains the short message "sorry unable to attend today, Hughes". Written on the back of the telegram and subsequently crossed out are some proposed minutes for a meeting that were never entered in the minute book. They reveal the difficulty in getting a good crew: "Proposed by C. R. Kelly that it is impossible to get a crew from Ardglass and that it is also impossible to get a better Killough crew". Another note states "Proposed by Dr McComisky [that] that three of Ardglass coastguard be substituted for three of the least capable of crew, seconded by General Brown". Finally, there is evidence that the cox Daniel O'Prey was still one of the main problems: "Dr McComisky [proposed] that the cox be reinstated but that he be seriously admonished by General B and also the same to crew and that the Institution be asked to give six months to have crew made more efficient and the district inspector ask[ed] that four exercises be given in that time".

Alas, it was of no avail. The last meeting of the committee took place on October 18th 1914. Lieut. Rigg and his assistant Lieut. Innis were there to report on an exercise on the previous night. The committee consisted of Clarence Craig, Mr. Finley, Mr Gillett and C. Russell Kelly. Lieut. Rigg stated that "he was not at all satisfied with the cox or crew, that the cox did not take charge of his men and would not give orders". Lieut. Rigg must have told them that the station was beyond redemption and was to be finally closed down. The last futile lines of the minutes of the meeting record that "a vote was taken as to whether the station should be kept open and was carried unanimously. Mr Craig asked for a vote to be taken on keeping present crew in boat. This was also carried". The minutes were never signed as the committee never met again.

YAWLS AT KILLOUGH, COUNTY DOWN

H C MADILL

Taylor's Yawl beached near Scordon (Courtesy of Down County Museum)

Details of the construction and layout of the yawl Marian B13 are described within the general context of yawl fishing at Killough from the early nineteenth century until its disappearance in the 1970s. Included are the recollections of Harry Henvey who remembers the working days of these yawls from the 1930s through to the end.

The village of Killough lies on the west side of the small Killough Bay which faces south-east into the Irish Sea. As soon as the wind might veer past south-southwest, however, the bay becomes sheltered by St John's Point a mile further west, and even in southerly or southeasterly wind a number of water rocks in the entrance to the bay absorb much of the wave force. Therefore the drying harbour, in the inner reaches of the bay, remains comparatively sheltered behind its piers.

The original little town of Killough and its quay was developed only during the early eighteenth century by the Ward family, as independent Irish Sea access to their adjacent estates. In the 1820s substantial further piers and wharves were built, and until the 1850s the harbour carried on a considerable trade, mostly grain exports and coal imports.[1]

A fishery report of 1822 by Alexander Nimmo for the Commissioners of Irish Fisheries[2] noted Killough's commercial activity and its involvement in the summer herring fishery. (The adjacent deep-water harbour of Ardglass was the centre for the fleets which converged at that time of the year on the north Irish Sea grounds.)

For Killough, Nimmo recorded:

> It is a considerable port for the corn and coal trade, having 15 carrying vessels; it is also engaged in the fishery, 18 smacks and wherries, and during the herring-fishing is much frequented by wherries from other places. It has also the only salt-works in the neighbourhood.

However, all this activity at the harbour appears to have been largely irrelevant to the year-round fishing carried on by small yawls. This was centred at Scordon, half a mile to seaward of the commercial harbour, where the boats used a gravelly beach sheltered from the east and south behind a rocky foreshore. Nimmo noted:

> There are 22 yawls which pursue the line fishery for haddock, cod, blockens etc. on the Rigg and East bank, about two miles from the harbour, and afford the chief supply of white fish to the county of Down; they use a small cove without a pier, where they can be readily launched into deep water by a slip which has been lately improved for their convenience.

In this yawl fishing the actual town and harbour at Killough appeared only to serve as a focus for the fishermen's dwellings and a possible first market for their catch.

Some 14 years after the Nimmo Report there is another glimpse into the fishing, in a 1836 Report into the Inquiry into the State of the Irish Fisheries.[3] There was then no mention of Killough vessels taking part in the Irish Sea herring fishery. It may well have been, with the continuing development of deep-water Ardglass, that tidal Killough was merely being used as a servicing and fish marketing overspill for the visiting fleets. However the yawl fishery was still active. The report noted that Killough had 20 of these boats each with five crew, and there was critical comparison between Killough yawl men and those who fished from Ardglass. Whereas many of the Ardglass men also had small plots of land and fished only three months of the year – making them 'neither good fishermen nor farmers' – of those fishermen at Killough only three had small farms and very few even had gardens. The Killough men, therefore, were nearly totally dependent on their boats, either fishing or acting as pilots for the harbour.

DIPPING LUG SAIL
AS DRAWN   11·6 sq m
           125 sq ft

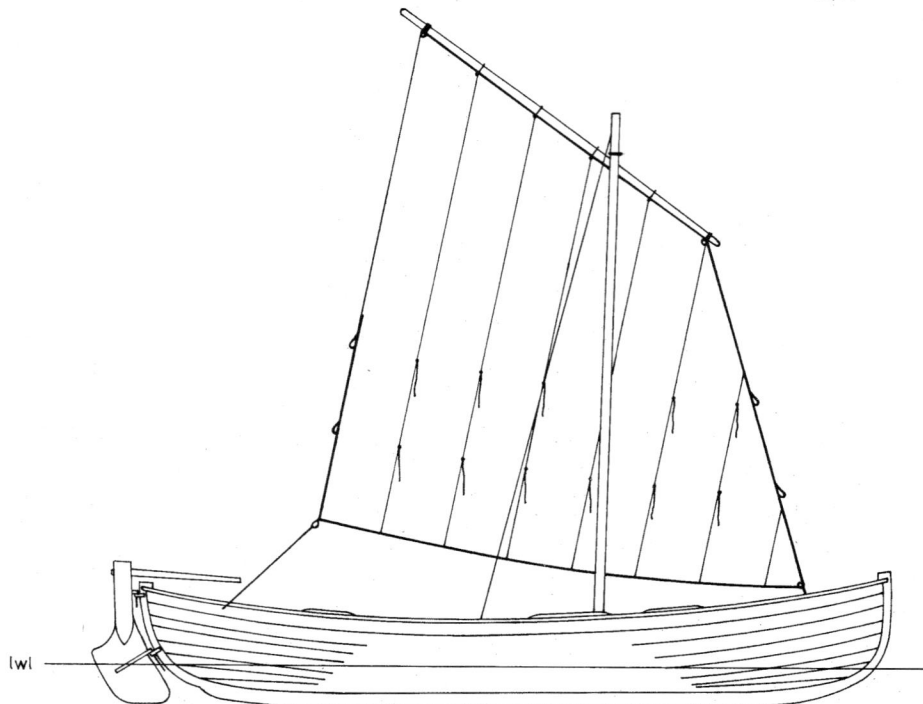

lwl

metres   0   1   2   3   4   5

KILLOUGH CO. DOWN
YAWL SAILING RIG

106

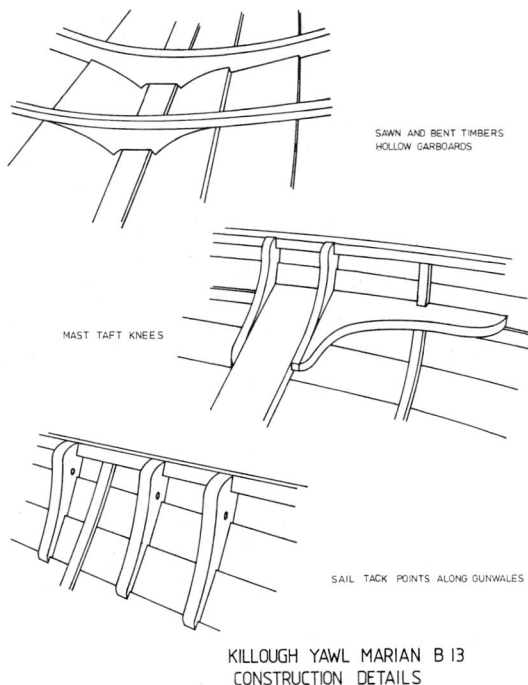

SAWN AND BENT TIMBERS
HOLLOW GARBOARDS

MAST TAFT KNEES

SAIL TACK POINTS ALONG GUNWALES

KILLOUGH YAWL MARIAN B 13
CONSTRUCTION DETAILS

"The Killough fishermen are almost always out…"

Evidence given in this 1836 Inquiry specifically describes these Killough boats as 'Norway Yawls'. Michael McCaughan has constructed a map of Ireland on which he located all similar Report references to Norway Yawls.[4] This gives a distribution of them as the principal coastal boat type continuously from Malin Head to Fair Head and down the east coast to Dublin Bay. For Ardglass the yawls were described by one source quoted in the 1836 Report as:

> …built with fir timber, about 20 feet keel, 6 feet beam, rowing 4 oars and costing from £5 to £7.

This description was repeated and expanded a little further by the Coastguard at Portrush on the north coast of County Antrim:

> They are alike at both ends, and very low in the centre; in length, twenty feet; breadth, six feet; depth, two feet four inches.[5]

Michael McCaughan points out that the Norway Yawl boat type first came to Ireland during the eighteenth century through importation of Norwegian-built boats brought in with cargoes of Scandinavian timber. He dates the end of such boat imports to the years following 1804, when the Norwegian timber trade with Britain became greatly reduced as a victim of the economic wars which ran in parallel to the military wars with Napoleon's Europe.

But even when Norwegian boats were still being imported it seems likely that Irish builders were also supplying a significant proportion of demand, and that the boats which they produced were based on the model of their Norwegian-built competitors in shape, performance and price. When imports ceased local builders on the north and east coasts continued to build, largely independently of each other, but both still producing the essentials of the Norway pattern demanded by their customers as 'the proper boat'.

On the north coast of Ireland the Norwegian elevation shape was modified with straighter stem and stern, and less gunwale sheer; but

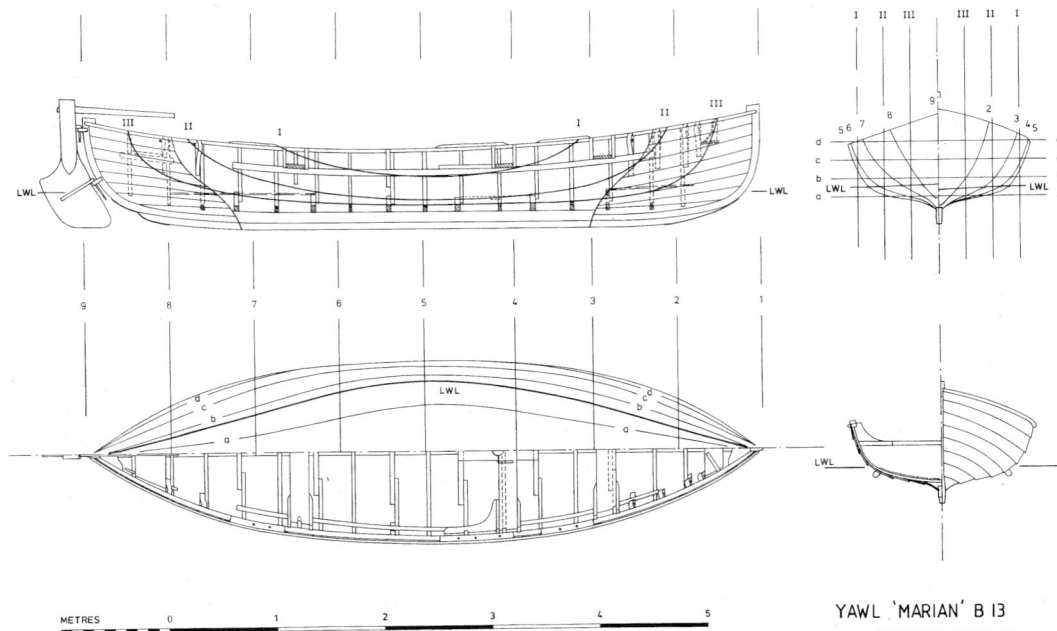

YAWL 'MARIAN' B 13

BUILT BY JAMES MURNAN KILCLIEF 1924
FOR MR ROBERT TAYLOR KILLOUGH CO. DOWN

6·29 x 1·74 x 0·60 m   (20' 7¼" x 5' 8½" x 1' 11¾")

METRES   0   1   2   3   4   5

constructionally the builders still maintained their own fabricated version of the Norwegian general flanged keel section,[6] and its separation from any direct support of the transverse frame timbers.[7] In County Down building the elevation shape followed more closely the Norwegian rounding of the ends, and in the maintaining of the lively sheer line. Constructionally too County Down remembered Norwegian practice in forming the curved-section of garboards by carving out of the solid, and in following the rabbeted keel tradition - although this latter detail is not a uniquely south Norway building feature.[8]

Differences also evolved in naming the boat type along different lengths of the coast. A skiff in County Louth and south Down was a yawl in the remainder of County Down north of Dundrum. A yawl east of Bengore Head in County Antrim (which the Ballintoy or Rathlin fishermen might even describe as a shallop, sloop, lateen, schooner, smack or wherry depending on the sailing rig), was a drontheim - that echoing of past Norwegian sources again - from Bengore Head to Malin Head. As transplanted later into the remainder of Donegal, and south into Connacht, it was described in official terminology as the Greencastle yawl. As regards rigs the east coast boats generally used a single-masted lug, and the north and later the west coast boats two-masted sprit sails.[9]

But despite this individualism the nineteenth century differences in east and north coast hull development were not differences of principle or concept, only of fine detail. New owners, throughout, continued to demand open, double-ended boats, clinker built, fine lined for easy working under oar or sail, light and strong enough to be launched off the foreshore. This was what the original Norwegian boats had provided and this is what the local building continued to give.

Although Killough as a small commercial port had been in decline from the mid-nineteenth century,[10] the 1911 edition of the *Irish Coast Pilot* for seamen was still noting its activity. "It is much resorted to by coasters and by fishing vessels in the herring season." The same comment was repeated in the 1930 edition, but with a caution: "…the west pier affords the best shelter …but it was reported in 1926 to be unsafe."

In 1928[11] the government declined to undertake major repair of the pier and during the 1930s trade had declined to a coal boat once a month and export of perhaps a couple of cargoes of potatoes and a cargo of grain once a year. At the beginning of the second World War what turned out to be the last cargo of Whitehaven coal was landed, and the 1941 edition of the Irish Coast Pilot was now warning any further potential users that "…both piers were in 1936 in a dilapidated state." And so after 200 years of use Killough's little port had melted away.

But all through this long decline the yawl fishing continued at Scordon. In 1926, 12 boats

were still alive, seven full-time employing 18 men, and five part-time with eight men. Two boats were laid up. A government study carried out in 1928 into the state of Northern Ireland fishing shows that, despite working only under oar and sail, the value of whitefish and pot catches from this 12 boat yawl fleet was very significant in comparison with the non-herring catches of the other County Down harbours, where engine-power and trawling was now making inroads.[12]

From this table (which was prepared from 1926 data) Killough, apparently, was landing the greatest value of lobster/crab of all the County Down harbours, and its overall highest earning value of catch per boat would indicate the commitment of its fishing community.

The yawl *Marian*, surveyed in 1998 after being laid up for some years, was one of that Killough fleet. It had been built in 1924 by James Murnan of Kilclief for Robert Taylor of Killough, fisherman and harbour pilot, and was registered as a new boat B13 in the Belfast district on the 9th of April 1924.

Fishing from a Killough yawl in the 1920s

Port	Boat Numbers			£ Catch/Value			Average Catch
	Full	Part	Total	Lobster/ Crab	Whitefish	Total	£ Value Per Boat
Donaghadee	6	16	22	86	1568	1654	75
Ballywalter	9	14	23	225	774	999	43
Portavogie (Boats mainly in herring fishing)				459	847	1306	
Portaferry/Strangford	6	40	46	0	280	280	6
Ardglass (Boats mainly in herring fishing)				65	1920	1985	
Killough	7	5	12	555	696	1251	104
Newcastle	8	8	16	7	906	913	57
Annalong (Boats mainly in herring fishing)				181	95	27600	
Kilkeel (Boats mainly in herring fishing)				72	100	172	

Value in catches in County Down, Report of 1928.

At 6.29m (20'7") length overall it was typical of the Killough yawl size, which the registry shows ranged generally between 5.5-6.7m (18'-20'). The beam of 1.74m (5'9") was of the traditional narrow proportion but maintained well over the centre third of the boat. The plan shape is quite symmetrical fore and aft at gunwale level with the fine entry waterlines even a trace finer at the sternquarters. In elevation the ends are well rounded; the curved stem and stern posts extend 1.0-1.5m (3'3"-5') inward from the vertical before joining into the straight keel.

The hull is planked in eight clinker-fastened strakes. The midships section has the top two boards forming a uniformly-flared topside with the definite bilge turn taking place in the next three boards. From there the uniform 10° minimum moulded deadrise floor[13] is produced with the next two boards and this finally leads to the more steeply-angled garboard strake beside the keel. This garboard is of the traditional south Down hollow section. It appears to have been fashioned out of 178 x 22mm (7" x 7/8") stock with 10mm (3/8") hollowing from the centre of the outside and taken also from the edge faces of the inside, to leave a uniform 12mm (1/2") curved section strake. This is set into the keel rabbet at a minimum chord deadrise of 28° (for which the deadrise of the rabbet slot face required to be 38° to accommodate the inside rounding). With the bilges immersed at the normal load waterline and with the amount of draft produced by the wineglass garboard layout, this body section gives a good combination of stability and weatherliness for the fine-shaped, easily-driven hull. The north coast drontheim section may have had a little more overall beam but its bilges were slacker.[14]

In construction the stems are fashioned out of 60 sided x 120mm (2³/8" x 4³/4") oak and scarfed to a 60 sided x 65mm (2³/8" x 2⁵/8") larch keel. Beneath this is fastened a further 62mm (2¹/2") depth of beach keel. Although this boat presently has protecting steel keelstrip only locally bow and stem, all the yawls working from the rough foreshore had full-length steel protection from bow to stern.

Planking is 11mm (⁷/16") thick spruce, copper rooved along the landings. The garboards and strake-ends are hooded and deadnailed into the keel and stem rabbets; no inside aprons were used. The bilge planking is protected by 2m (6'6") long wooden bilge keels fastened along the lower edge of the 4th strake from the gunwale.

Transverse timbers are alternately bent larch, and a combination of sawn elm floors with side-lapped bent larch futtock pieces running to the gunwales. The bent larch is of 32 sided x 20mm (1¹/4" x 1³/4") section, and where used from gunwale to gunwale has a short elm filler piece from garboard to garboard so that there is a smooth curvature possible across the keel. In the composite timbers the sawn elm floors are of 45 sided x 32mm minimum thickness (1³/4" x 1¹/4"), joggled to give a close fit over keel and strakes. The larch futtock

extensions are lapped to the floors by an average of 200mm (8"). Skin fastening to the bent timbers is by rooved copper nails; to the sawn floors by deadnailing. In all cases the sawn floors or filler pieces under the bent timbers rest on and are securely fastened to the keel, with substantial limberholes for drainage provided at each side of the keel. (In north coast drontheim building where the timbers span clear across the keel, the fishermen refer to the resulting large limberhole as 'the gutter')

Gunwales are 45 moulded x 35mm (1³/4" x 1³/8") larch, tapered bow and stern to be held between substantial oak breasthooks. The outside edge of the top strake is protected by a wooden rubbing strip, with some lengths locally along the top of the gunwales protected by half-round steel strips.

The yawl presently contains 3 rowing tafts with a clear space between the middle and aft tafts where a portable 'slip taft' could be set when more seating then stowage space was needed. The mast heel

Killough Yawl under sail, painting by Johnnie McSherry, 1885

Launch of the Sweet Scordon, June 19th 1998

originally fitted into a step mounted on top of the floor timbers, the mast held against the after side of the middle taft by a metal collar. This taft was specially supported by oak lodging and standing knees, the other tafts and seats only by standing knees. Each of the 3 rowing tafts rest on a light 55 x 10mm (2¼" x ³/₈") wearing fastened to the timbers, with rowing rowths bored for twin thole pins fitted on top of the gunwale adjacent to each.

Close to the bow is a small beam and close to the stern a small seat for the helmsman. The standing knees are of a form particular to south Down in that instead of being through-fastened onto the flat of the taft they are only deadnailed into the sides of the beam. Fastening to the gunwales, however, is in the normal through-riveted form.

The yawl clearly was intended for sailing as well as rowing because the builder included on it 4 alternative tack strong-points attached to each gunwale between the bow and the forward rowing taft, to suit a variety of wind directions and reefing patterns for the dipping lugsail. For making fast the halliard, another strong-point is fastened to the gunwale each side at 3 frames aft of the mast, and for sheet control 2 holes with inside strengthening are provided both sides through the top strake, adjacent to the aft steering seat.

Floorboards in the body of the boat between the 3 rowing tafts are laid in panels directly onto the timbers and follow the skin curvature. Forward and aft of this the floorboards are laid in flat panels supported on horizontal floor joists.

The outside colour scheme has the 3 top strakes maintained white as originally. The lower 5 strakes presently are painted light grey, but this appears to be an overcoating of an original green colour. Inside, the top 2 strakes and the taft ends are maintained white, with the gunwales and remainder of the tafts picked out in light grey. The inside bilges appear to have been tarred originally; presently they too have been painted light grey.

In its transition from pulling/sailing to outboard engine the yawl dispensed with the original rudder, and the top of the sternpost was modified to take an outboard bracket. The rudder shown on the drawing is as recalled by Harry Henvey of St John's Point

Sweet Scordon under sail, 1999

from his days growing up in Killough between the 1930s and the 1950s. The sail plan drawing has also been prepared from his recollections, together with the placing of the various sailing fitments still existing on the yawl.

'I remember there being up to 10 pulling and sailing yawls at Scordaun before the war and up to about 1950. There was very little fishing during the war because the usual ground was in a firing-range area and was closed. But the fishing started off again after the war.

The boats were all kept at Scordaun, pulled up on the gravel beach above the high watermark. None was kept afloat so they didn't need their bottoms antifouled. The topsides inside and out were painted generally a light colour but the bilges inside were tarred and the bottom outside would be tarred or red-leaded.

The yawls were worked up and down to the water on greased wooden sticks, about 3ft long of 3" by 1½" set out about 4ft apart. Two men could launch a boat down the slope of the shore, but it could take 3 or 4 to bring them back up. At low water spring tide it could be up to 100 yards from the water, even up to 70 yards at low water neaps; so it could be quite a pull'.

Most of the yawls were worked full-time by their crews, when the weather allowed. None had any land. While Killough harbour was still working Bob Taylor in *Marian* and Alex O'Prey in the *St Bernard* were also pilots and used their own boats for boarding steamers. But there were other owners too; I remember Dan and Desmond O'Prey in the *Alexander* and Sam Simmons in the *Snowdrop* and Willie Ross in the *Excelsior*. And then there were other fishing families with boats; George Small in the *Kate* and Paddy Burns in the *Mannix*, and Sammy McSherry. Willie Ross still lives in Killough.

The summer fishing from April to the end of September was inshore working pots from Killough Bay, and round St John's Point to Dundrum bar with 2 man crews. In July and August there could be handlining for mackerel too, when they would come in; and some boats might jig lines for herring or drift short nets if there were signs of them being close to the shore. But it was never like the Mourne herring fishing at Kilkeel.

The winter fishing was handlines and long lines for cod and haddock from

October to April. At times the yawls with up to 6-man crews might even go 10 to 15 miles south or south-west of St John's Point to fish. If the wind didn't suit to set a sail then 4 men at a time would take spells in rowing. The oars were about 10 to 12 feet long. For sailing, the boats carried a dipping lug and would stow 3 or 4 half cwt. bags of sand under the mast and aft rowing tafts for ballast. The rope tail in the tack of the sail was made up to one of the tack points on the weather gunwale. The halliard to hoist the yard was passed through a sheave or a dumb sheave in the mast head, and the fall made fast to an eye on the weather gunwale aft of the mast. When the boat was tacked the halliard was eased so that when the sail tack was undone and brought round behind the mast, then there was enough slack to dip

Building Sweet Scordon at Harry Henvey's boat shed at St John's Point

Yawls of Scordon, painting by Johnnie McSherry, 1885

the heel of the yard and to make the sail tack up again on the new weather gunwale. The single sheet rope then had to be unreeved and lead from the outside into the new leeside fairlead hole aft, beside the helmsman. If the wind got up there were 2 sets of reef points for shortening sail. When the boat was just being rowed then the mast was taken down and stowed with its heel under the mast taft and its head 5 or 6 feet over the bow.

The yawls worked with oar and sail up to the early 1950s but gradually many of the sterns were altered to take Seagull outboard engines; though Bob Taylor's boat worked all her days at Killough just as she had been built. After the 1950s any new boat that came had a square stern.'

When Bob Taylor and his brother Willie decided to retire from fishing in the 1970s the Taylor family yawl *Marian* was sold to Robert Fitzpatrick of Minerstown, about three miles west of Killough, where it continued to be worked off the shore fishing pots until 1988. It was during this time that the stern was altered to take an outboard engine. After the owner's death the boat was donated by the Fitzpatrick family to Down County Museum who recognised its value as one of the last yawls once so common on the coast. In particular it represented the long history of the Killough fishing community, which because of its lack of facilities had been unable to make the transition from a fishing trade to a fishing industry. Since 1993 it has been in temporary storage under cover at Castleward, courtesy of the National Trust. After 74 years this boat is still in remarkably good condition and easily capable of being restored for museum display, her working days long over.

But the yawl tradition is not dead, for a replica of *Marian* has just now been built at St John's Point by Harry Henvey and Harry Magee for the Palatine Trust with a grant of money from the European Regional Development Fund. The Trust intends to rig its new yawl and to stimulate general interest in relearning the art of working it again from Killough, under its dipping lug sail.[15]

A W Brøgger has written about the continuity of boat culture in Norway over the past 1000 years:

'...The most interesting feature in this building of smaller boats, which thus maintained itself for hundreds and hundreds of years, untouched by wars, changes of kings and dynasties, higher political developments of every kind, is this deep substratum of folk-culture. The big ships vanished with the wars and the Norwegian royal line. The little boats

Scordon with yawls, painting by Johnnie McSherry, 1885

remained indissolubly bound up with the life of the peasantry … The peasant boat-builders conserved the full harvest of that vast social effort which is linked with the Norwegian boat.'[16]

Some 240 years ago, perhaps, the Norway yawl entered Irish coastal culture also and was similarly conserved. Despite the inroads of industrialisation, where small wooden boats are yet being built in the northern half of Ireland there is still much of this Norwegian clinker heritage unconsciously within what is believed to be 'the proper boat'.

References, Sources and Acknowledgments

PART ONE:

BIBLIOGRAPHY

Bassett G.H. County Down Guide of 1886

Harris W. The Ancient and Present State of County Down 1774

O'Laverty Rev T. The Diocese of Down and Connor 1878

Wilson W. Shipwrecks of the Ulster Coast

Teer G. A Killough Historian and Storyteller

Reeves. Ecclesiastical Antiquities of Down, Connor and Dromore 1897

Knox. History of County Down 1875

Green E.R.R. Industrial Archaeology of County Down 1963

Stevenson J. Two Centuries of Life in Down 1920

Seward. Topographical Dictionary of Ireland 1795

Lewis. Topographical Dictionary of Ireland 1837

Pender. Census of Ireland 1659

Magee J. Lecale in the 16th and 17th Centuries

Healy M. Killough: Past, Present and Future

Lecale Miscellany. Lecale Historical Society

U.A.H Society. East Down

Griffiths. Evaluation of Tenements 1863

National Trust. Castleward

Small G. Sweet Dreams; The Life and Works of Rex McCandless

Parliamentary Gazeteer of Ireland 1846

County Down Handbook

Ulster Towns

Downpatrick Recorder 1836-1956

ACKNOWLEDGMENTS

Agnes George.

Harry Henvey.

George Johnson.

Daniel Laird.

Anne Maynes.

Mary Ellen McIlmale.

Brendan McIlmale.

Emmett Small.

Patrick Small.

Jack Stewart.

Anthony Teague.

Philomena Waish.

Gerard Walsh.

Henry Walsh.

Margaret Wyatt.

Downpatrick Library Staff.

S E E L B Headquarters Ballynahinch.

And all the people of Killough who contributed to this book.

PART TWO:

The soldiers tale is based on the journal that was in the possession of the late Cecily Parkinson-Cumine. The sailor's tail is based on the letters written by James Cumine-Parkinson to his mother in Killough and were also in the possession of the late Cecily. The development of the early pier at Killough is based on the letters between Francis Lascelles and Judge Michael Ward which are preserved in the Public Records Office of Northern Ireland (D.2092/1/1/58 - D.2092/1/6/148).

The essay on the early schools is based on the most part from the Ordnance Survey Memoirs published by the Institute of Irish Studies, QUB, and school records preserved in the Public Record Office of Northern Ireland (ED/6/1/3/3). The section on the Sheil's almshouses is based on reports in the Downpatrick Recorder and the Charles Sheils Parliament Act of 1864. The report on the Killough lifeboat is based on records in the possession of Mrs Mary Duffy, Killough.

PART THREE:

REFERENCES

1. R. H. Buchanan, 'The Irish Sea: the geographical framework' in Michael McCaughan and John Appleby (eds) *The Irish Sea: aspects of maritime history* (Belfast 1989) p9.

2. Fourth Report of Commissioners of Irish Fisheries, 1822, *House of Commons Papers*, 1823 (383) x .409.

3. First Report of the Commissioners of Inquiry into the State of the Irish Fisheries 1836, *House of Commons Papers* 1837 (77) xxii. 53-55.

4. Michael McCaughan, 'Double-ended and clinker built. The Irish dimension of a European boat-building tradition' in Alan Gailey (ed) *The Use of Tradition* (Cultra 1988) p34.

5. See note 3, 1836 Report, p73.

6. For flanged and rabbeted keel forms see – Sean McGrail *Ancient Boats in North West Europe* (London 1987) pp112-115; A. Osler, *The Shetland Boat* (National Maritime Museum Monograph 58, London 1983) pp52-54. This details the making of a flanged keel from the solid. A. Christensen (ed), *Inshore Craft of Norway*, based on the work of Bernard and Øystein Faerøyvik (Greenwich 1979). Where boat section drawings are included, the flanged keel form appears to be indicated on 19 out of the 20 small boats under 9m overall length. Only in a single case (from south Norway) is a rabbeted keel shown. For the general situation, however, see p31, '...the (south-)eastern boat builders used rabbets in keel and stem, while the western and northern boat builders worked with a T-shaped keel and unrabbetted stems...'

7. For separation of frame timbers and keel in Norwegian boat construction see – McGrail *Ancient Boats* p145, '...in the Viking boatbuilding tradition no find has yet been recorded with frames fastened to the keel...'; Osler *The Shetland Boat*, Fig. 21 clearly shows the similar Shetland tradition. In Christensen, *Inshore Craft* ...all the boat section drawings, including that for the rabbeted keel, indicates an arching of the frame timber over the keel without direct support one to the other.

8. Christensen, *Inshore Craft* ...pp16,18 'Within living memory, most of the types of western and northern Norway (boats) were built with axe-hewn garboards, even in districts where sawn timber was abundant.

9. Local naming of the boat type –

    a. A. Teggarty, Kilkeel, 22 March 1996: '…Co Louth and here was 'skiff' country. A yawl in Kilkeel was a small square-sterned punt, anything over 10 to 12 feet, that the nickey boats carried as drive boats…'

    b. H. Henvey, St John's Point, 18 Feb 1998.

    c. Newry Fishing Boat Registers 1869-1930, Public Record Office of Northern Ireland CUS/3/ 6/3/1,3.

    d. Belfast Fishing Boat Registers 1902-1950, Public Record Office NI CUS/1/6/3/1,2

    e. Coleraine Fishing Boat Register 1902-1939, Merchant Shipping Agency Cardiff.

    f. Londonderry Fishing Boat Registers 1871-1915, CUS/2/6/3/1,2.

10. R. H. Buchanan, ibid. p10.

11. Request for improvements to Killough harbour 1926-28, Public Record Office NI D/2720/1

12. Report of the Departmental Advisory Committee on the Development of Fishing Harbours in Northern Ireland 21st Feb 1928, Public Record Office NI COM/42/2. This provides the data on boats, men and catches used in the given table.

13. McGrail, *Ancient Boats* p114 quotes definitions proposed by Eric McKee to describe various amounts of floor deadrise; 0-7° flat floor, 7°-11° raised floor, more than 11° vee floor. The 10° deadrise found on this yawl would therefore fall at the upper end of the proposed 'raised floor' middle category.

14. Garboard deadrise –

    a. Christensen, ibid. Of the twenty 18th to 20th century Norwegian boats under 9m (30 feet) length for which midship section drawings are included, the measured minimum garboard deadrise is in the range 15°-45°, the overall average is 22°. This Killough yawl garboard chord deadrise of 28° (deadrise of the upper face of the rabbet 38°) is slightly more than the average of the sample of boats included in Faerøyvik.

    b. *The building and trials of the replica of an ancient boat; the Gokstad faering*, (National Maritime Museum Monograph 11, London 1974). Garboard deadrise in the 9th century Gokstad faering is 20° for the 6.5m boat.

15. Maurice Hayes' book *Sweet Killough Let Go Your Anchor* (Belfast 1994) gives a wonderful flavour of Killough village, its activities and its community in the 1930s, through the all-observing eyes of the author growing up there as a small boy.

16. A. W. Brøgger and H. Shetelig *The Viking Ships* (Stanford 1953).